MW00928525

April 2012

Thank you for purchasing the High School and Mental Health Curriculum. This curriculum was first developed in 2009, and through user feedback has continued to evolve.

This most recent version of the guide no longer includes a media CD, instead, we have loaded the support files onto our website for the user to download to their computer and/or use directly from the website.

The support materials are located on:
http://teenmentalhealth.org/curriculum/support-materials/

The username is: **resource_user**
The password is: **t33nh3alth**

This includes videos, powerpoint slides, handouts and teachers training materials. We are developing of an eLearning Centre, which will become a permanent home for these resources and others, and will include a discussion forum for teachers to share ideas about mental health in the classroom.

The team also continues to post new resources on the website teenmentalhealth.org under the Educators tab, as well as on:

teenmentalhealth.org/curriculum

One of our recent updates includes a virtual classroom that was developed in partnership with Taking It Global to supplement the curriculum guide. You can find information about this free online classroom at:

http://teenmentalhealth.org/for-educators/virtual-classroom/

Thank you for your patience and particpation as we continue to try new ways to connect with teachers and students.

We look forward to continue working with you.

Table of Contents

Background

About CMHA

The Canadian Mental Health Association (CMHA), founded in 1918, is one of the oldest voluntary organizations in Canada. Each year, it provides direct service to more than 100,000 Canadians through the combined efforts of more than 10,000 volunteers and staff in over 135 communities across Canada.

As a nation-wide, voluntary organization, the Canadian Mental Health Association promotes the mental health of all and supports the resilience and recovery of people experiencing mental illness. The CMHA accomplishes this mission through advocacy, education, research and service.

"Our Vision is Mentally Healthy People in a Healthy Society"

The Canadian Mental Health Association focuses on combating mental health problems and emotional disorders. Our tools include research and information services, sponsored research projects, workshops, seminars, pamphlets, newsletters and resource centres.

The CMHA's programs assist with employment, housing, early intervention for youth, peer support, recreation services for people with mental illness, stress reduction workshops and public education campaigns for the community.

In addition, the CMHA acts as a social advocate to encourage public action and commitment to strengthening community mental health services and legislation and policies affecting services. All our mental health projects are based on principles of empowerment, peer and family support, participation in decision-making, citizenship, and inclusion in community life.

CMHA National
595 Montreal Road, Suite 303
Ottawa, ON K1K 4C2

Tel: (613) 745-7750
Fax: (613) 745-5522

www.cmha.ca

Educating young people about mental health and mental illness

Having access to reliable information on positive mental health and mental illness is crucial for high school students for a number of reasons. Mental and emotional problems are common among high school students and need to be addressed, just like students' physical health problems.

Even if students have not experienced mental illness, it is very likely that they know someone who has. Consider the following statistics to get an idea of just how widespread the effects of mental illness are in society, and among young people in particular:

1) Mental illness is second only to heart disease as the leading cause of disability in Canada and worldwide. *(Global Burden of Disease – World Health Organization, World Bank, Harvard University, 1990)*

2) Mental health problems affect one in every five young people at any given time.

3) The first symptoms of severe, chronic forms of mental illness (such as schizophrenia, bipolar disorder, depression and anxiety disorders) generally appear between the ages of 15 and 24. *(CMHA, 2003)*

4) An estimated two-thirds of all young people with mental health problems are not receiving the help they need.

5) Suicide is the third leading cause of death among young people aged 15-24. At least 90% of those who commit suicide have a diagnosable mental illness. Learning about mental illness and the importance of seeking treatment can save lives.

6) Fear of stigma and the resulting discrimination discourages individuals and their families from getting the help they need. *(SAMHSA, 2004)*

The modules in this guide present fundamental information about mental health and mental illness. Students can apply the knowledge they gain from this guide as they encounter new situations and make decisions about their lives.

The Role of Secondary Schools

Secondary schools provide an ideal environment and natural opportunities to address issues of mental health and illness. Educators can play an important role by delivering accurate, comprehensive information and by challenging the stereotypes about mental illness held by the general community.

The **Mental Health and High School Curriculum** program encourages secondary schools to actively promote the message that seeking help is a sensible and supportive act rather than a sign of weakness or a breach of loyalty. Therefore, in addition to providing information and education about mental health and mental illness, this material actively promotes discussion about when, why, how and where to seek help.

Reference: *The Science of Mental Illness*, National Institute of Mental Health, 2006.
http://science-education.nih.gov/supplements/nih5/mental/guide/nih_mental_curr-supp.pdf

Brief History of the Mental Health & Highschool Curriculum Project

The roots of this pilot and evaluation project go back a long way within the Canadian Mental Health Association (CMHA), National Office. For the past twenty-five years, in accordance with our Framework for Support model for mental health and recovery, CMHA has directed much of its energy into exploring the ways people with mental illness and mental health problems can live full and productive lives in community.

For youth specifically, some of our initiatives have engaged communities to take early action on first-episode psychosis, others support young people to find mainstream employment; and still others have helped universities and colleges understand how to accomodate students with psychiatric disabilities. In 2003-4, with funding from the Government of Canada's Social Development Partnerships Program, Human Resources and Skills Development Canada, we developed tools for students, their teachers and parents to help them deal with mental health problems in high school.

The same funder subsequently supported the development of a curriculum guide for high schools in 2006-7, under the leadership of Project Manager Catherine Willinsky, with indispensible contributions from Dr. Sonia Chehil, Dr. Stan Kutcher, and youth at Laing House in Halifax, Nova Scotia. The need to test the guide in actual classrooms was the impetus for this latest phase of the project--a rigorous evaluation inititative involving CMHA branches in four sites across Canada: Barrie and Hawkesbury Ontario; Medicine Hat, Alberta; and Truro, Nova Scotia.

With continuing leadership support from Dr. Stan Kutcher, the evaluation team from University of Ottawa, and the youth at Laing House, and with strong guidance from Project Manager Heather Bruce, the project trained teachers to deliver the curriculum, tested the results in high schools in the pilot sites, and made the necessary adjustments. Teachers suggested changes that would help it meet their classroom realities and their students' needs; students told us how to make it more relevant to their interests and their lives. This revised Curriculum Guide is the result of all these efforts.

It has been a privilege for me, as the former CMHA National Director of Programs and Research, to see the evolution of this work from its seeds in the Framework for Support policy model to the new High School Curriculum Guide we have today. I hope it will make a difference for students, teachers and parents across the country as we all continue to learn how to nurture and protect our mental health.

Bonnie Pape
Project Advisor

A note from the Sun Life Financial Chair in Adolescent Mental Health (SLFC)

This version of the **Mental Health and High Schools Curriculum** Guide is the result of an ongoing collaboration between the Canadian Mental Health Association and the Sun Life Financial Chair in Adolescent Mental Health at Dalhousie University and the IWK Health Centre (Halifax, NS). The revised curriculum incorporates suggestions and advice received from a pilot test at four different Canadian high schools and continues to be based on the best available scientific evidence and current understandings regarding mental health and mental disorders in young people.

This revised curriculum would not have been possible without the orgainzational leadership of Heather Bruce (CMHA), the pilot training participation of Melanie Kelly (IWK), the evaluation framework developed by Dr. Ron Melchers and Lindsey Pecaric of the University of Ottawa, and the curriculum revisions created by Shelley LeBlanc, Yifeng Wei, David Venn and Christina Carew from the SLFC Team, which I was pleased to provide with ongoing oversight and quality ascertainment.

Curriculum users are encouraged to access the website of the Canadian Mental Health Association (www.cmha.ca) and the Sun Life Financial Chair in Adolescent Mental Health (www. teenmentalhealth.org) for further information pertaining to youth mental health.

Dr. Stan Kutcher

The Pilot and Evaluation Project
(June 2008 - March 2009)

If you had asked me, "Will you be Project Manager for a national high school pilot project in a few years?" while I was in the hospital being treated for mania, I would've said, "Er, now you're the delusional one here..." And yet here I am!

Mostly because Alex Keay at CMHA National Office thought of me, when they were looking for someone to pilot their new high school curriculum. For a former high school teacher now working for CMHA Ottawa branch in public education, this was a wonderful and daunting opportunity. I'm eternally grateful to those that became my sherpas as I climbed that learning cliff, and to those that had faith that I could do it. I just might end up saving the world after all, one student at a time.

I'd like to dedicate this guide to my son Adrian and all the young people making their way through this tough thing we call life. May it offer them some compassion, some hope, and the inspiration to make their mental health a priority.

Heather Bruce, Project Manager

In memory of my father Lou Bruce, 1933 - 1985, who took his life, and gave me the passion to do this work.

Sincere thanks to the following people, who dedicated much of their time and energy to the success of this project.

Our amazing piloting teachers, schools, and their students:
Renée Lacelle, École secondaire catholique de Casselman, ON
Alicia Eliot, Barrie Collegiate, ON
Shaughna Ainsworth and Wendy Speers, Young Parents Program, Barrie Collegiate, ON
Tim Taylor and Sean Rogers, Alternative Program, Barrie Collegiate, ON
Janay Rittinger, Eagle Butte Secondary School, Medicine Hat, AB
Wayne Garden, Hants East Rural High School, Truro, NS
David Clarke, Central Colchester Junior High School, Truro, NS
Kate Adams, Cobequid Educational Centre, Truro, NS
Mike Boyle, LSK First Nations School, Indian Brook, NS

Our superb CMHA branch coordinators:
Aleta Armstrong, Barrie-Simcoe, ON
Mallory Boileau, Hawkesbury, ON
Debbie Dolliment, Medicine Hat, AB
Jackie Murphy, Truro, NS

Our brilliant Project Advisory Network members:
Bonnie Pape, Project Advisor
Catherine Willinsky, Consultant

Our entire CMHA National Office, of quality not quantity:
Dr. Taylor Alexander, Executive Director
Laura Evans, Administrative Assistant
David Alge, Financial Manager
Paige Vieyra, Webmaster
Branka Gudelj, Fundraising Manager
Alex Keay, Guardian Angel
Julie Flatt, Project Manager, Routes to Work

The stellar Sun Life Financial Chair in Adolescent Mental Health and his team at the IWK Health Centre in Halifax:
Dr. Stan Kutcher, Sun Life Financial Chair
Tracy Mackenzie, Administrative Assistant
Amy MacKay, Administrative Assistant
Melanie Kelly, Cofacilitator for the teacher training sessions
Yifeng Wei, Project Coordinator
Shelley Leblanc, Educational Consultant
David Venn, Public Relations
Christina Carew, Public Affairs Advisor

Our terrific evaluation team at the University fo Ottawa's Centre for Research and Evaluation of Community Services (CRECS):
Tim Aubry, Director
Dr. Ron Melchers, Professor of Graduate Program in Evaluation
Lindsey Pecaric, Graduate Student
Marita Wagner

Our traslator magnifique at TranslatArt:
Sylvain Jobin

Our website wizards:
Rick Nigol, CEO, eLearn Campus (original site)
Jon-Anthony Lui, eLearn Campus (original site)
Headspace Design, TeenMentalHealth.org

Our geniuses at The Printing House Ltd. in Ottawa:
Mark Madsen-Russell, Manager
Darrell Kennedy, Manager

Our fabulous colleagues at Laing House in Halifax:
Shaleen Jones, Executive Director
Ron Patterson
Lisa Armstrong
Ross Macleod

Our kind friends at TopDrawer Creative:
Rachael Muir
Kerry Smiley

Our helpful advisors at the CMHA Provincal Offices:
Michelle Gold, Ontario
Tom Shand, Alberta
Carol Tooton, Nova Scotia
Renée Ouimet, Quebec

Également offert en français sous le titre:
La santé mentale et l'école secondaire : Guide de formation

This publication is also available on the Internet at the following addresses:
www.teenmentalhealth.org/curriculum

This publication can also be made available in alternate format(s) upon request.

This project is funded by the Government of Canada's Social Development Partnerships
Program, Human Resources and Skills Development Canada. The opinions and
interpretations in this publication are those of the author and do not necessarily reflect
those of the Goverment of Canada.

Introduction Part 1

This guide has been developed to accompany another resource, Mental Health and High School (www.cmha.ca/highschool) which contains information for secondary school students who are experiencing mental health problems, and for their parents and educators.

The Mental Health and High School Curriculum Guide

This section provides general information on the material and ways that it can be used in the classroom. You will find specific suggestions in the instructions provided with each module.

The **Mental Health and High School** materials have been developed in recognition of the need to address the mental health of young Canadians by providing teacher and student-friendly classroom based resources.

The tools in this package, (including the Curriculum Guide, PowerPoint presentations and a three-part video) are designed to help teachers and other members of school staff to:

• Promote students' awareness of mental health issues and reduce the stigma
associated with mental illness;

• Provide a safe and supportive environment in which all students can maximize
their learning;

• Remain accessible and responsive to students' needs;

• Help students develop their abilities to cope with challenges and stress;

• Identify those students in particular need of assistance or support.

By using the activities in the curriculum guide, teachers and students will explore the language of mental health and mental illness and learn about the causes, symptoms and approaches for dealing with different mental illnesses such as mood, anxiety, eating and psychotic disorders. Through the audiovisual materials, students will hear directly from other young people about their experiences with mental illness, and the impact of stigma on their personal struggles and at the community and societal level.

Students will also learn about seeking help and providing peer support and meaningful recovery from mental illness, as well as the importance of positive mental health for all.

Why use the guide?

Stigma, fear and a lack of information about mental health problems have been identified as reasons why mental health and mental illness have not been adequately addressed in many schools. The **Mental Health and High School** materials have been developed to help overcome some of these barriers. By providing accurate, peer-reviewed information on mental health and mental illness, and a range of interactive activities, the guide can help teachers deliver crucial information in a way that engages and challenges youth.

Many of the curriculum guidelines for senior-level courses in Health and Physical Education contain explicit requirements for mental health education. The **Mental Health and High School Curriculum** Guide provides teachers with a user and student-friendly way of meeting the learning objectives and curriculum requirements.

Objectives

> The Mental Health and High School Curriculum Guide has several objectives.

- To provide secondary school staff across Canada with consistent, reliable and easy-to-use information to help promote basic understanding of mental health and mental illness in the classroom;

- To provide students with a basic introduction to normal brain functioning to help them better understand mental health and mental illness;

- To help students understand the various factors that can contribute to mental illness, and the biological component which makes mental illnesses not that different from other illnesses;

- To equip teenagers with the knowledge they need in order to identify when they, a friend or family member is experiencing mental health problems or mental illness;

- To reduce the stigma associated with mental illness by providing clear, factual information about mental illness, its causes, ways to address it and recovery;

- To help young people understand that seeking help for mental health problems is very important, and to suggest strategies for seeking help;

- To reinforce the importance of positive mental health and effective ways of coping with stress;

- To provide information about recovery from mental illness, and the factors which help keep people well.

Where does the material fit into the curriculum?

Each province and territory has developed its own distinct curriculum frameworks, including specific courses, content standards and learning expectations, this unit has been designed to be general enough to meet many of the different criteria for Health and Physical Education courses across Canada.

This guide is designed for use in Grades 9 through 12. Although the material is intended primarily for use in Health and Physical Education courses, it may also fit well with a number of other curriculum areas, including: Personal Development, Family Living, Child Studies, Psychology and Sociology.

Educational approach

The **Mental Health and High School Curriculum** Guide uses activities and other strategies which engage young people in their learning, and challenge them to explore the issues.

The modules in this guide are comprehensive, easy to implement and fun. The interactive teaching strategies used in the activities provide opportunities for building students' skills in participation, communication, relationship-building, teamwork, and critical thinking. Many of the activities in the modules are designed to be completed by teams of students working together.

The activities address a range of learning styles by incorporating both experiential and reflective elements, and using guided discussion to assist students to process and share new experiences and information.

The modules include both print-based classroom activities and audio-visual activities (web-based). The modules are designed to fit into 50 minutes of classroom time. Each module is written in the form of lesson plans that can be easily implemented by teachers without additional training.

Teacher tips are provided to highlight the sensitive aspects of certain modules, and offer suggestions about strategies that are designed to teach about as well as model mental health.

Teachers can integrate their assessment of student learning through this resource with their assessment plan for the course with which they are using these materials.

Implementing the curriculum guide

1)   Before implementing the curriculum guide it is strongly recommended that teachers review the teacher training unit and complete the self test. (Self test is also available online at teenmentalhealth.org/curriculum

2)   Before teaching the modules the students should be given the student questionnaire which will be given again after the modules are taught as a sort of pre and post test evaluation.

The six modules are designed to stand alone, or to be taught in sequence so that students progress from: 1) the stigma of mental illness to 2) an understanding of the basic functions of the brain to 3) details about different types of mental health problems and mental illnesses and their treatment, to 4) a real-life look at young people's experiences of mental illness, to 5) the importance of services and ongoing support for those living with mental illness, to 6) ways that everyone's mental health can be enhanced and supported through positive coping strategies and stress-reduction.

Module	Major Concepts
Module 1: The stigma of mental illness	• Stigma acts as a barrier to people seeking help for mental health concerns • Learning the facts about mental illness can help dispel misconceptions and stigma • People's attitudes about mental illness can be positively influenced by exposure to accurate information • We all have a responsibility to fight the stigma associated with mental illness
Module 2: Understanding mental health and mental illness	• Everyone has mental health regardless of whether or not they have mental illness • The brain controls our feelings, thoughts and behavoiurs • A mental illness is a health condition that changes a person's thinking, feelings or behaviour (or all three) and that causes that person distress and difficulty in functioning • Mental illnesses have complex causes that include a biological basis and are therefore not that different from other illnesses or diseases. As with all serious illnesses, the sooner people get help and effective treatment for mental illness, the better their long and short-term outcomes
Module 3: Information on specific mental illnesses	• Mental illness describes a broad range of mental and emotional conditions. The type, intensity, and duration of symptoms vary

cont.>

Implementing the modules (cont.)

Module	Major Concepts
Module 3 (cont.): Information on specific mental illness	• The exact cause of mental disorders is not known, but most experts believe that a combination of factors-biological, psychological and social--are involved • Like illnesses that affect other parts of the body, mental illnesses are treatable and the sooner people get proper treatment and support, the better the outcomes
Module 4: Experiences of mental illness	• Mental illnesses are diseases that affect many aspects of a person's life • Mental illnesses are usually episodic. With appropriate support and treatment, most people can function effectively in everyday life • Getting help early increases the chances that a person will make a full recovery from mental illness • Mental illnesses, like physical illnesses, can be effectively treated
Module 5: Seeking help and finding support	• There are many ways of seeking help for mental health problems and mental illnesses, and resources are available within schools and within broader community • Knowing the signs and symptoms of mental illness helps people know how to distinguish the normal ups and downs of life from something more serious • Recovery from mental illness is possible, when a range of supports, beyond formal treatment, are available • Everyone has mental health that can be supported and promoted, regardless of whether or not they also have mental illness
Module 6: The importance of positive mental health	• Positive coping strategies can help everyone maintain and enhance their mental health

Implementing the modules (cont.)

2) Format of the modules:

As you review the modules, you'll find that each one includes several key features:

- The Overview provides a short summary of the activity;

- The Learning Objectives lists specific understandings or abilities students should derive from completing the modules;

- The Major Concepts section presents the central ideas that the module is designed to address;

- Teacher Background provides ideas about suggested information to review prior to leading the module to enhance your understanding of the content so that you can confidently facilitate class discussions, answer students' questions and provide additional examples and illustrations;

- The Activities section provides a list of the steps which comprise the module, and suggested timelines;

- The Required Materials section provides a list of the masters (overheads and information sheets) that will be needed to complete the activities in each module;

- The In Advance section provides instructions for collecting and preparing materials required to complete the activities in the module. This includes preparing materials (such as photocopies and overheads from the masters provided), and reviewing audiovisual material;

- Each Activity has its own Purpose, which provides a brief explanation of the activity, and a how to section, which breaks the activity down into simple, easy-to-follow steps;

- Notes to Teachers appear as sidebars. Look here for information about issues that may be confusing or that need to be emphasized.

Introduction

Mental disorders affect approximately 15-20 percent of Canadian youth and about 70% of these disorders begin prior to age 25 years. It is therefore highly likely that educators will be faced with having to deal with young people who are experiencing or living with mental illness. In order to assist educators in their work, the team has created the following mental health education module specifically designed to help inform educators about some of the most common mental disorders found in young people. This resource is meant to be used in conjunction with the **Mental Health and High School Curriculum** Guide for teachers to review or upgrade their knowledge about mental disorders. It can also be used as a resource for classroom use if so desired.

-- *Dr. Stan Kutcher*

Activities

Activity 1: Self-evaluation (before reviewing material)
Activity 2: View Powerpoint presentation: Teacher Training
Activity 3: Read Mental Health Training for Teachers booklet
Activity 4: Self-evaluation (after reviewing material)
Activity 5: Correction of self-evaluations and comparison

Materials required -- *all materials for activities can be found at:*
http://teenmentalhealth.org/curriculum/teacher-training/

*   Self-evaluation handout
*   PowerPoint presentation: Teacher Training
*   Booklet: Mental Health Training for Teachers
*   Correction key for self-evaluation

Activity 1: Self-evaluation (before reviewing material)

1. Take the self-evaluation questionnaire (30 questions) and answer each question either true or false. (Note: make a copy of this quiz or write your answers elsewhere as you will do this quiz two times, alternatively you can also take it online at:

    http://teenmentalhealth.org/curriculum/teachertraining/

2. Put the questionnaire aside until you've finished reviewing the teacher training materials.

Activity 2: View PowerPoint presentation: Teacher Training

1. Access Supplementary Resources at: **http://teenmentalhealth.org/curriculum/teacher-training/** view the Teacher Training PowerPoint presentation (96 slides in total).

2. Take as much or as little time as you need or want.

Activity 3: Read Mental Health Training for Teachers booklet

1. Read through the booklet, which is designed to be used as a reference in the classroom. There is some overlapping material from the PowerPoint, but it is presented in an entirely different way.

Activity 4: Self-evaluation (after reviewing material)

1. Take the self-evaluation questionnaire (30 questions) again and answer each question either true or false. Don't look at your first questionnaire answers.

Activity 5: Correction of self-evaluations and comparison

1. Use the answer key and correct your questionnaires.
2. Compare the two results. Hopefully you did better the second time around.

Optional: Teacher training workshop

Should you wish to have a teacher training workshop at your school or school board, please contact the team by visiting us online at: **http://teenmentalhealth.org/for-educators/training-programs/**
or contacting us at: **info@teenmentalhealth.org**

Self-evaluation for teachers

Activity 1: Before reviewing material
Activity 4: After reviewing material

1. A phobia is an intense fear about something that might be harmful (such as height, snakes).

    a. true   b. false

2. Useful interventions for adolescent mental disorders include BOTH psychological and pharmacologic treatment.

    a. true   b. false

3. Mental distress can occur in someone who has a mental disorder.

    a. true   b. false

4. Stigma against the mentally ill is uncommon in Canada.

    a. true   b. false

5. Substance abuse is commonly found together with a mental disorder.

    a. true   b. false

6. The most common mental disorders in teenage girls are eating disorders.

    a. true   b. false

7. The stresses of being a teenager are a major factor leading to adolescent suicide.

    a. true   b. false

8. Three of the strongest risk factors for teen suicide are: romantic breakup, conflict with parents, and school failure.

    a. true   b. false

9. Schizophrenia is a split personality.

    a. true   b. false

10. A depressed mood that lasts for a month or longer in a teenager is very common and should not be confused with a clinical depression that may require professional help.

    a. true   b. false

11. Teen suicide rates have decreased over the last decade in North America.

    a. true   b. false

Self-evaluation for teachers

Activity 1: Before reviewing material
Activity 4: After reviewing material

12. Diet, exercise and establishing a regular sleep cycle are all effective treatments for many mental disorders in teenagers.

    a. true   b. false

13. Anorexia nervosa is very common in teenage girls.

    a. true   b. false

14. Bipolar disorder is another form for manic depressive illness.

    a. true   b. false

15. Many clinical depressions that develop in teenagers come "out of the blue".

    a. true   b. false

16. Obssessions are thoughts that are unwanted and known not to be correct.

    a. true   b. false

17. Serotonin is a liver chemical that helps control appetite.

    a. true   b. false

18. Mental disorders may affect between 15-20 percent of Canadians.

    a. true   b. false

19. Most people with panic disorder do not get well with treatment.

    a. true   b. false

20. Depression affects about 2 percent of people in North America.

    a. true   b. false

21. A psychiatrist is a medical doctor who specializes in treating people who have a mental illness.

    a. true   b. false

Self-evaluation for teachers

Activity 1: Before reviewing material
Activity 4: After reviewing material

22.   Attention Deficit Hyperactivity Disorder (ADHD) is equally common in boys and girls.

        a. true   b. false

23.   A hallucination is defined as a sound that comes from nowhere.

        a. true   b. false

24.   Panic disorder is a type of Anxiety disorder.

        a. true   b. false

25.   Medications called "anti psychotics" are helpful to treat the symptoms of schizophrenia.

        a. true   b. false

26.   A delusion is defined as seeing something that is not real.

        a. true   b. false

27.   Lack of pleasure, hopelessness and fatigue can all be symptoms of a clinical depression.

        a. true   b. false

28.   Nobody with schizophrenia ever recovers.

        a. true   b. false

29.   People with mania may experience strange feelings of grandiosity.

        a. true   b. false

30.   Mental disorders are psychological problems caused by poor nutrition.

        a. true   b. false

(See answer key end of this section)

Teacher self evaluation answer key

1.	True	16.	True
2.	True	17.	False
3.	True	18.	True
4.	False	19.	False
5.	True	20.	False
6.	False	21.	True
7.	False	22.	False
8.	False	23.	False
9.	False	24.	True
10.	False	25.	True
11.	True	26.	False
12.	False	27.	True
13.	False	28.	False
14.	True	29.	True
15.	True	30.	False

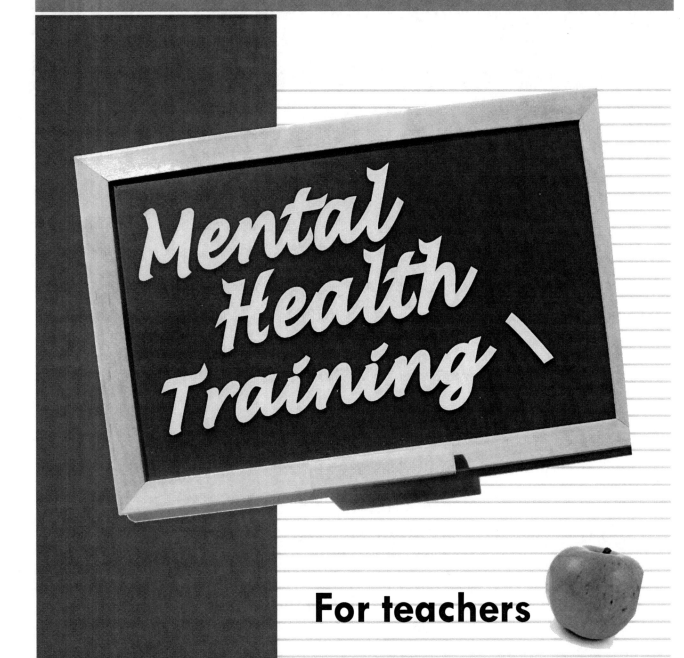

For teachers

October 2008 version

Chehil, LeBlanc and Kutcher ©
Sun Life Financial Chair in Adolescent Mental Health Group

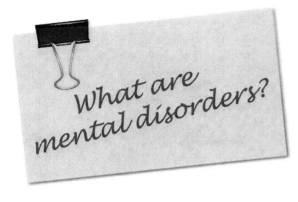

What are mental disorders?

Here's what we know about mental disorders:

- Disturbances of emotion, thinking, and/or behaviour
- May occur spontaneously (without a precipitant)
- Severe (problematic to the individual and others)
- Lead to functional impairment (Interpersonal, Social)
- Prolonged
- Often require professional intervention
- Derive from brain dysfunctions – brain disorder
- Is rarely, if ever, caused by stress alone

Mental disorders are NOT:

- It is not the consequence of poor parenting or bad behavior.
- It is not the result of personal weakness or deficits in personality
- It is not the manifestation of malevolent spiritual intent
- Only in exceptional cases is it caused by nutritional factors
- It is not caused by poverty.

How is the brain involved?

- The brain is made up of: cells, connection amongst the cells and various neurochemicals
- The neurochemicals provide a means for the different parts of the brain to communicate
- Different parts of the brain are primarily responsible for doing different things (eg: movement)
- Most things a brain does depends on many different parts of the brain working together in a network

WHAT HAPPENS INSIDE THE BRAIN WHEN IT GETS SICK?

- A specific part of the brain that needs to be working on a specific task is not working well
- A specific part of the brain that needs to be working on a specific task is working in the wrong way
- The neurochemical messengers that help different parts of the brain communicate are not working properly

HOW DOES THE BRAIN SHOW IT'S NOT WORKING WELL?

- If the brain is not working properly, one or more of its functions will be disturbed
- Disturbed functions that a person directly experiences (such as sadness, sleep problems, etc.) are called SYMPTOMS
- Disturbed functions that another person sees (such as over activity, withdrawal, etc.) are called SIGNS
- BOTH signs and symptoms can be used to determine if the brain may not be working well
- The person's usual life or degree of functioning is also disrupted because of the signs and symptoms

Mental disorders are associated with disturbances in six primary domains of brain function:

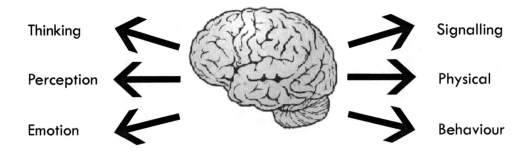

Thinking

Perception

Emotion

Signalling

Physical

Behaviour

When the brain is not functioning properly in one or more of its six domains, and person experiences problems that interfere with his or her life in a significant way, they may have a mental disorder.

BUT...
Not all disturbances of brain functioning are mental disorders. Some can be a normal or expected response to the environment – for example: grief when somebody dies or acute worry, sleep problems and emotional tension when faced with a natural disaster such as a hurricane.

What's the difference between mental distress and mental disorders?

Distress:
Common; caused by a problem or event; usually not severe (may be severe); usually short lasting; professional help not usually needed; professional help can be useful;
DIAGNOSIS NOT NEEDED.

VS.

Disorders:
Less common; may happen without any stress; often with high severity; usually long lasting; professional help usually needed.
NEEDS TO BE DIAGNOSED.

What causes mental illness?

A variety of different insults to the brain can lead to mental illness. Basically there are TWO major causes that can be independent or can interact:

24

GENETICS (the effect of genes on brain development and brain function) and

ENVIRONMENT (the effect of things outside the brain on the brain — such as infection; malnutrition; severe stress; etc)

Classification of Mental Disorders:

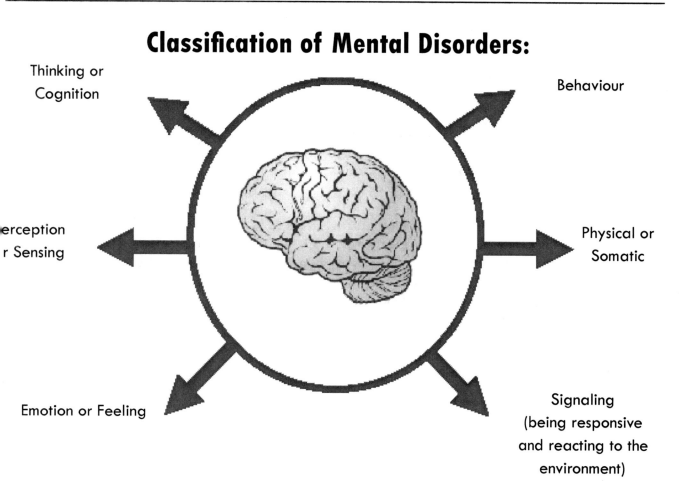

Thinking or Cognition

Behaviour

erception r Sensing

Physical or Somatic

Emotion or Feeling

Signaling
(being responsive
and reacting to the
environment)

Mental Disorders of Thinking & Cognition: (Psychotic disorders)

WHAT ARE PSYCHOTIC DISORDERS?

Psychotic disorders are a group of illnesses characterized by severe disturbances in the capacity to distinguish between what is real and what is not real. The person with psychosis exhibits major problems in thinking and behavior. These include symptoms such as delusions and hallucinations. These result in many impairments that significantly interfere with the capacity to meet ordinary demands of life. Schizophrenia is an example of a psychotic disorder that affects about 1% of the population.

Who is at risk for developing Schizophrenia?

Schizophrenia (SCZ) often begins in adolescence and there often may be a genetic component although not always. A family history of SCZ, a history of birth trauma and a history of fetal damage in utero increases the risk for SCZ. Significant marijuana use may bring on SCZ in young people who are at higher risk for the illness.

What does Schizophrenia look like?

Delusions are erroneous beliefs that may involve misinterpretation of experiences or perceptions. One common type of delusion is persecutory (also commonly called paranoid) in which the person thinks that he or she is being harmed in some way by another person, force or entity (such as God, the police, spirits, etc.). Strongly held minority religious or cultural beliefs are not delusions.

Hallucinations are perceptions (such as hearing sounds or voices, smelling scents, etc) that may occur in any sensory modality in the absence of an actual sensory stimulus. They can be normal during times of extreme stress or in sleep like states. Occasionally they can occur spontaneously (such as a person hearing their name called out loud) but these do not cause problems with everyday life and are not persistent.

Thinking is disorganized in form and in content. For example, the pattern of speaking may not make sense to others or what is being said may not make sense or be an expression of delusional ideas.

Behavior can be disturbed. This can range from behaviors that are mildly socially inappropriate to very disruptive and even threatening behaviors that may be responses to hallucinations or part of a delusion. Self-grooming and self-care may be also compromised.

A young person with schizophrenia will also demonstrate a variety of cognitive problems ranging from difficulties with concentration to "higher order" difficulties such as with abstract reasoning and problem solving. Most people with schizophrenia will also exhibit what are called "negative symptoms" which include: flattening of mood; decreased speech; lack of will.

A person with schizophrenia may exhibit delusions, hallucinations and disordered thinking (also called "positive symptoms") as well as negative symptoms at different times during the illness.

What are the criteria for the diagnosis of Schizophrenia?

1 – positive symptoms as described above (delusions, hallucinations, disorganized thinking)
2 – negative symptoms as described above
3 – behavioral disturbances as described above
4 – significant dysfunction in one or more areas of daily life (social, family, interpersonal, school/work, etc.)
5 – these features must last for at least 6 months during which time there must be at least one month of positive symptoms

What can I do if it is SCZ?

A young person with SCZ will require immediate effective treatment – usually in a specialty mental health program (first onset psychosis program). If an educator suspects SCZ a referral to the most appropriate health provider should be made following discussion with the parents about the concerns.

What do I need to watch out for?

Many young people with SCZ will demonstrate a slow and gradual onset of the illness – often over the period of 6 – 9 months or more. Early signs include: social withdrawal; odd behaviors; lack of attention to personal hygiene; excessive preoccupation with religious or philosophical constructs; etc. Occasionally the young person suffering in the prodrome may exhibit very unusual behaviors – often in response to a delusion or hallucinations. Sometimes it may be difficult to distinguish the onset of SCZ (also called a "prodrome") from other mental disorders – such as depression or social anxiety disorder. Young people suffering from the prodrome of SCZ may also begin abusing substances – particularly alcohol or marijuana and develop a substance abuse disorder concurrently. Occasionally the young person may share bizarre ideas or may complain about being persecuted by others or may appear to be responding to internal voices. Rarely these delusions or hallucinations may be accompanied by unexpected violent acts.

Questions to ask?

Can you tell me what you are concerned about? Do you feel comfortable in school (your class)? Are you having any problems thinking? Are you hearing or seeing things that others may not be hearing or seeing?

Mental Disorders of Emotion and Feeling: (Mood disorders)

There are two types of mood disorders which include unipolar mood disorders and bipolar mood disorders. Unipolar disorder is major depression, where as bipolar disorder is when a person experiences cycles of depression and mania.

DEPRESSION

Not to be confused with the word "depression" which is commonly used to describe emotional distress or sadness, depression means CLINICAL DEPRESSION, which is a mental disorder.

What are the different types of Depression?

There are two common kinds of clinical depression, Major Depressive Disorder (MDD) and Dysthymic Disorder (DD). Both can significantly and negatively impact on people's lives. They can lead to social, personal and family difficulties as well as poor vocational/educational performance and even premature death due to suicide. Additionally, patients with other illnesses such as heart disease and diabetes have an increased risk of death if they are also diagnosed with depression. This is thought to be due to the physiologic affects that depression has on your body as well as lifestyle effects such as poor self care, increased smoking and alcohol consumption. Individuals with clinical depression usually require treatment from health professionals but in mild cases may experience substantial improvement with strong social supports and personal counseling.

What do MDD and DD look like?

MDD is usually a life-long disorder beginning in adolescence or early adulthood and is characterized by periods (lasting months to years) of depressive episodes that are usually self-limiting. The episodes may be separated by periods (lasting months to years) of relative mood stability. Sometimes the depressive episodes may be triggered by a negative event (such as the loss of a loved one; severe and persistent stress such as economic difficulties or conflict) but often the episodes may occur spontaneously. Often there is a family history of clinical depression, alcoholism, anxiety disorder or bipolar (manic-depressive) disorder. DD is a low grade depression that lasts for many years. It is less common than MDD.

What is a depressive episode?

A depressive episode is characterized by three symptom clusters: 1.mood 2.thinking (often called cognitive) and 3.body sensations (often called somatic). MDD may present differently in different cultures, particularly in the somatic problems that people present with. Symptoms:

- Must be severe enough to cause functional impairment (stop the person from doing what he or she would otherwise be doing, or decrease the quality of what they are doing)
- Must be continuously present every day, most of the day for at least two weeks
- Can not be due to a substance or medicine or medical illness and must be different from the persons usual state

These symptoms are:

Mood:
- Feeling "depressed"; "sad"; "unhappy" (or whatever the cultural equivalent of these descriptors is)
- Feeling a loss of pleasure or a marked disinterest in all or almost all activities
- Feelings of worthlessness, hopelessness or excessive and inappropriate guilt

Thinking:
- Diminished ability to think or concentrate or substantial indecisiveness
- Suicidal thoughts/plans or preoccupation with death and dying

Body Sensations:
- Excessive fatigue or loss of energy.
- Significant sleep problems (difficulty falling asleep or sleeping excessively)
- Physical slowness or in some cases excessive restlessness
- Significant decrease in appetite that may lead to noticeable weight loss

Criteria:

FIVE of the above symptoms must be present EVERY DAY for MOST OF THE DAY during the same two week period; ONE of the FIVE symptoms MUST BE either depressed mood or loss of interest or pleasure.

Things to look for:

People with depression are at an increased risk for attempting suicide. Every person with depression should be monitored for suicide thoughts and plans. As a teacher you need to be aware that a depressed student who begins to talk about suicide needs to be referred to his/her health provider immediately.

What can I do if it is Depression?

You can identify the disorder and counsel the person with the disorder (including education of the person and family) if it is mild and if you are trained in counseling. If the disorder is more intense or the person is suicidal you should immediately refer the person to the health professional best suited to treat the depression. Ideally this should be done in collaboration and with the active support of the school guidance counselor or identified school based mental health provider. Once an intervention occurs and the young person is back at school it is important that you be part of the ongoing treatment team and help develop and address learning needs. You may also need to continue to provide realistic emotional support.

Questions to ask:

Have you lost interest or pleasure in the things that you usually like to do? Have you felt sad, low, down or hopeless? Are you feeling like ending it all? IF the student answers yes to either of these, further assessment of all of the symptoms should be directed to the appropriate health care sector.

BIPOLAR DISORDER

- Illness is characterized by cycles (episodes) of depression and mania
- Cycles can be frequent (daily) or infrequent (many years apart)
- During depressive or manic episodes the person may become psychotic
- Suicide rates are high in people with bipolar mood disorder

In Bipolar disorder how is 'mania' different from feeling extremely happy?

- Mood is mostly elevated or irritable
- Many behavioral, physical and thinking, problems
- Significant problems in daily life because of the mood
- Mood may often not reflect the reality of the environment
- Is not caused by a life problem or life event

Bipolar - What to look for:

- History of at least one depressive episode and at least one manic episode.
- Rapid mood changes including irritability and anger outbursts.
- Self-destructive or self-harmful behaviors – including: spending sprees; violence towards others; sexual indiscretions; etc.
- Drug or alcohol overuse, misuse or abuse.
- Psychotic symptoms including: hallucinations and delusions

Mental Disorder of Signaling: (The Anxiety Disorders)

WHAT IS GENERALIZED ANXIETY DISORDER?

GAD is described as excessive anxiety and worry occurring for an extended period of time about several different things. This persistent apprehension, worry and anxiety causes distress and leads to physical symptoms.

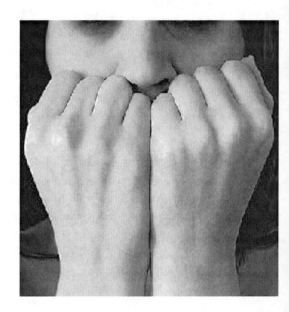

Who is at risk for developing GAD?

GAD often begins in childhood or adolescence and there is also a genetic or familial component. Once GAD is present, the severity can fluctuate and exacerbations often occur during times of stress. Other psychiatric disorders are also risk factors for GAD such as depression, panic disorder and agoraphobia.

What does Generalized Anxiety Disorder look like?

Generalized Anxiety Disorder (GAD) is characterized by excessive anxiety and worry about many different things. The worry is out of proportion to the concern or event. This anxiety and worry must be noticeably greater than the usual socio-cultural norms. Youth with GAD often do not present with panic attacks as in panic disorder. Often they present with physical complaints such as headaches, fatigue, muscle aches and upset stomach. These symptoms tend to be chronic and young people may miss school or social activities because of these physical symptoms.

How do you differentiate GAD from normal worrying?

Anxiety can be broken into four categories:

1) **Emotions** – i.e. feeling fearful, worried, tense or on guard.
2) **Body Responses** – anxiety can cause many different responses of the body including increased heart rate, sweating, and shakiness, shortness of breath, muscle tension and stomach upset.
3) **Thoughts** – when experiencing anxiety, people are more likely to think about things related to real or potential sources of danger and may have difficulty concentrating on anything else. An example is thinking something bad is going to happen to a loved one.
4) **Behaviours** – people may engage in activities that can potentially eliminate the source of the danger. Examples include avoiding feared situations, people or places and self medicating with drugs or alcohol.

When does anxiety become a disorder?

These physical, emotional and behavioural responses to perceived danger are normal reactions that we experience everyday. Many times this 'anxiety response' is automatic, and every creature has these automatic responses as a way of protecting themselves from danger. However, anxiety becomes a problem when:
- It is greater intensity and/or duration then typically expected given the context.
- It leads to impairment or disability in work, school or social environments
- It leads to avoidance of daily activities in an attempt to lessen the anxiety

What are the criteria for the diagnosis of GAD?

1. Excessive anxiety and worry occurring for at least 6 months about several things
2. Difficulty controlling the worry
3. The anxiety and worry are associated with 3 or more of the following:
    a. Restlessness or feeling on edge, fatigued, difficulty concentrating, muscle tension or sleep disturbance
4. Anxiety and worry are not due to substance abuse, a medical condition or a mental disorder
5. The anxiety and physical symptoms cause marked distress and significant impairment in daily functioning

What can I do if it is Generalized Anxiety Disorder?

The first thing is to identify the problem for the young person and elicit assistance from a helper knowledgeable about the problem. Some people with GAD will experience improvements in their anxiety and functioning with supportive cognitive based counseling. Others may require medication. Referral to an appropriate health professional for medical attention could be considered if the GAD is severe and if the functional impairment is extensive. For some, merely knowing that they have GAD and receiving supportive counseling may be helpful enough.

Things to look for:

Some people with GAD may go on to develop a clinical depression. Some people may begin to use substances such as alcohol to help control their anxiety. If this occurs, they may be at risk of developing a substance abuse or substance dependence problem.

Questions to ask?

Can you tell me about your worries? Do you or others see you as someone who worries much more than he/she should? Do you or others consider you to be someone who worries much more than most people do? Do you have trouble "letting go of the worries"? Do you sometimes feel sick with worry – in what way? What things that you enjoy doing or would like to do are made less enjoyable or are avoided because of the worries? What if anything do you find makes the worries better – is this for a short or a long time?

What is Social Phobia?

Social phobia, also known as Social Anxiety Disorder, is characterized by the presence of an intense fear of scrutiny by others, which may result in embarrassment or humiliation.

What does Social Phobia look like?

Young people with social phobia fear, doing something humiliating in front of others, or of offending others. They fear that others will judge everything they do in a negative way. They believe they may be considered to be flawed or worthless if any sign of poor performance is detected. They may cope by trying to do everything perfectly, limiting what they are doing in front of others and gradually withdraw from contact with others. Youth with social phobia often experience panic symptoms in social situations. As a result they tend to avoid social situations such as parties or school events. Some may have a difficult time attending class or may avoid going to school altogether. Although young people with social phobia recognize that their fears are excessive and irrational, they are unable to control it and therefore avoid situations that trigger their anxiety. The presentation of Social Phobia may vary across cultures and although it may occur in children it usually onsets in the adolescent years. It must not be confused with "shyness" and the strength of the fears may wax and wane over time.

What are the criteria for diagnosis of Social Phobia?

The following must be present for someone to have social phobia:

*   Marked and persistent fear of social or performance situations in which the person is exposed to unfamiliar people; fear of embarrassment or humiliation
*   Exposure to the feared situation almost always provokes marked anxiety or panic
*   The person recognizes that the fear is excessive or inappropriate
*   The avoidance or fear causes significant impairment in functioning and distress
*   The feared social or performance situations are avoided or else endured with intense anxiety or distress
*   The symptoms are not due to a substance, medicine or general medical condition

In children, Social Phobia may be expressed by crying, tantrums, and a variety of clingy behaviors. Other psychiatric diagnoses that Social Phobia must be differentiated from include: Panic Disorder; Pervasive Developmental Disorder; Schizoid Personality Disorder).

What can I do if it is Social Phobia?

The first step is the identification of the problem. Often, people with Social Phobia will have suffered for many years without knowing the reason for their difficulties. Sometimes just informing and educating them about the problem can be helpful, particularly in mild cases. Treatment is not indicated unless the problem is causing significant functional impairment but counseling using cognitive behavioral techniques and exposure to the anxiety-provoking situation in the company of a counselor may help the person better deal with their difficulties. If the disorder is severe, referral to an appropriate health care provider is indicated, and the counselor can provide ongoing support. A teacher may be able to assist in behaviour modification programs (such as getting used to a classroom situation). If you think a student may have social phobia it is important not to draw attention publically to their difficulties but speak with them in private about what you notice – be supportive.

What do I need to watch out for?

Some young people with Social Phobia will use excessive amounts of alcohol to help decrease their anxiety in social situations. In some cases, Social Phobia can be a risk factor for the abuse of alcohol or other substances. In young children it is important to differentiate Social Phobia from Pervasive Developmental Disorders such as Autism. Children with autism, in contrast to children with social phobia, will not demonstrate age-appropriate social relationships with family members or other familiar people.

Questions to ask

Do situations that are new or associated with unfamiliar people cause you to feel anxious, distressed or panicky? When you are in unfamiliar social situations are you afraid of feeling embarrassed? What kinds of situations cause you to feel that way? Do those feelings of embarrassment, anxiety, distress or panic stop you from doing things you would otherwise do? What have you not been able to do as well as you would like to do because of those difficulties?

WHAT IS PANIC DISORDER?

Panic Disorder is characterized by recurrent, unexpected, anxiety (panic) attacks that involve triggering a number of frightening physical reactions. The frequency and severity of panic attacks can vary greatly and can lead to agoraphobia (fear of being in places in which escape is difficult).

Who is at risk for developing Panic Disorder?

The onset of panic disorder is commonly between the ages of 15-25. People who have first-degree relatives with panic disorder have an 8x higher risk of also developing panic disorder themselves. Panic Disorder is associated with an area of the brain that regulates alertness. Disturbance in this area of the brain is one explanation for why panic attacks occur.

What does Panic Disorder look like?

Young people with Panic Disorder experience recurrent, unexpected panic attacks and they greatly fear having another attack. They persistently worry about having another attack as well as the consequences of having a panic attack. Some may fear they are 'losing their mind' or feel they are going to die. Often they will change their behaviour to avoid places or situations that they fear might trigger a panic attack. In time, the person may come to avoid so many situations that they become bound to their home.

What are the components of a panic attack?

The person has four of more of the following symptoms which peak within 10 minutes:

1. palpitations, pounding heart or accelerated heart rate
2. sweating
3. trembling or shaking
4. sensations of shortness of breath or smothering
5. feeling of choking

6. chest pain or discomfort
7. nausea or abdominal pain
8. feeling dizzy, unsteady, lightheaded or faint
9. feeling of unreality or being detached from oneself
10. fear of losing control or going crazy
11. fear of dying
12. numbness or tingling in the body
13. chills or hot flashes

What are the criteria for Panic Disorder?

Assessing panic disorder involves evaluating 5 areas:

1. Panic attacks
2. Anticipatory anxiety
3. Panic related phobic avoidance
4. Overall illness severity
5. Psychosocial disability

For a diagnosis of panic disorder, a patient must have:

1. Recurrent unexpected panic attacks
2. One or more of the attacks has been followed by ≥1 month of:
   - Persistent concern of having additional attacks
   - Worry about the implications of the attack or its consequences
   - A significant change in behaviour as a result of the attacks
3. Can be ± agoraphobia
4. Panic attacks are not due to substance abuse, medications or a general medical condition
5. Panic attacks are not better accounted for by another mental disorder

What can I do if it is Panic Attack?

The first thing is to identify the panic attack and provide a calm and supportive environment until the attack passes. Education about panic attacks and panic disorder is often very helpful and should ideally be provided by a professional with good knowledge in this area. Counseling using cognitive behavioral methods may be of help and medications can be used as well. The teacher's role in helping a young person suffering from a panic disorder can also involve assisting them in dealing with their anxieties about having another attack and also helping them with strategies to combat avoidance of social situations. Therefore it is a good idea for a teacher to be part of the treatment planning and treatment monitoring for a youth with panic disorder.

Things to look for:

Youth with panic disorder are at a high risk for developing depression. If the person appears sad or hopeless and has suicidal thoughts, a diagnosis of depression must also be suspected. Some young people with panic disorder may also develop substance abuse (particularly alcohol) and counseling around these issues is very important.

Questions to ask?

Can you describe in your own words what happens when you have one of these episodes (some people will refer to them as "spells")? How many of these episodes have you had in the last week, in the last month? What do these episodes mean to you? What do these episodes stop you from doing that you would otherwise usually do? What do you do when these episodes occur? Do you ever feel that you would like to be dead or think that your problem is so great that you should kill yourself? How do your family, friends, loved ones, etc. react to these episodes? What do they say is the problem?

OBSESSIVE COMPULSIVE DISORDER

Obsessive Compulsive Disorder (OCD) is an anxiety disorder characterized by obsessions and/or compulsions. Obsessions are persistent, intrusive, unwanted thoughts, images or impulses that the person recognizes as irrational, senseless, intrusive or inappropriate but is unable to control. Compulsions are repetitive behaviours, which the person performs in order to reduce anxiety associated with an obsession. Examples of these are counting, touching, washing and checking. Both can be of such intensity that they cause a great deal of distress and significantly interfere with the person's daily functioning. Obsessions are different from psychotic thoughts because the person knows that they are their own thoughts (not put inside their head by some external force) and the person does not want to have the thoughts. Compulsions are different from psychotic behaviors because the person knows why he/she is doing the activity and can usually say why they are doing them.

Who is at risk for developing OCD?

OCD often begins in adolescence or early adulthood, although it can start in childhood. It is quite common and affects both men and women. First-degree relatives of people with OCD are more likely to develop OCD. It is important to note that people with OCD are at higher risk for developing depression and other anxiety disorders.

What does OCD look like?

OCD should not be confused with superstitions or those repetitive checking behaviors that are common in everyday life. They are not simply excessive worries about real life issues. A person with OCD will have significant symptoms of either obsessions or compulsions or both. These symptoms will be severe enough to cause marked distress, are time consuming (take up more than one hour per day) and significantly interfere with a person's normal activities (work, school, social, family, etc.).

Obsessions:
- Recurrent and persistent thoughts, impulses or images that are experienced as intrusive and not appropriate and cause significant distress or anxiety
- These symptoms can not be simply excessive worries about everyday life
- The person with these symptoms tries to suppress or ignore them. The person may try to neutralize, decrease or suppress the thoughts with some other thought or action.
- The person knows that the thoughts are coming from his/her own mind.

Compulsions:

- Repetitive behaviors (such as checking, washing, ordering) or mental acts (such as counting, praying, repeating words silently) that the person feels driven to perform in response to an obsession or according to rigid rules
- These behaviors or mental acts are aimed at preventing or reducing distress or preventing some dreaded event or situation BUT are not realistically connected to the obsessions they are meant to neutralize

How do you differentiate between OCD and Psychosis?

This is a very important step to take if you suspect someone has OCD. In general, patients with OCD have insight into the senselessness of their thoughts and actions and often try to hide their symptoms. This distinguishes OCD from psychotic disorders such as schizophrenia because those patients lack any insight into the senseless nature of their symptoms.

What can I do if it is OCD?

You can educate the student about OCD and how it is treated. If the symptoms are associated with impairment (social or academic) you should send the student to the school guidance or health professional who can then refer the person to the professional best suited to provide treatment and you can continue to provide education and support to the student if that is mutually agreed to. Often young people will be treated with cognitive behavioral therapy (CBT). Sometimes this may require a teacher's input. It is important to know if any academic modifications need to be made to enhance learning opportunities for young people with OCD so including the teacher in treatment planning and treatment monitoring is usually necessary.

Things to look for:

There are two main things to watch out for. The first is the possibility that the symptoms could be part of a psychosis. Therefore it is very important to rule out a psychosis disorder. [PLEASE REVIEW THE SECTION ON PSYCHOSIS] The second thing to watch for is the effect OCD has on the young person's classmates. Sometimes students with severe OCD will try to involve their classmates (or their teachers) in their compulsions. If this happens then it can cause significant problems at school. Educating yourself about OCD and the importance of not participating in the OCD rituals important.

Questions to ask:

Are you having thoughts that are coming into your mind that you do not want to be there? Can you tell me what those thought are? Do those thoughts cause you to feel uncomfortable or anxious or upset? Do you think that those thoughts are true? Where do you think those thoughts are coming from? How are you trying to deal with or stop the thoughts from coming? What do the thoughts stop you from doing that you would otherwise be doing? How much of the time are those thoughts on your mind?

Please describe the things that you are doing that are causing distress to you or other people. Can you tell me why you are doing those things? What do you think will happen if you do not do those things? What do those things that you are doing stop you from doing that you would otherwise be doing? How much time do you spend doing those rituals?

WHAT IS POST TRAUMATIC STRESS DISORDER?

Post Traumatic Stress disorder (PTSD) develops after a trauma occurs that was either experienced or witnessed by the patient. It involves the development of psychological reactions related to the experience such as recurrent, intrusive and distressing recollections of the event. These may be in the form of nightmares, flashbacks and/or hallucinations.

Who is at risk for developing PTSD?

Not all people who have experienced a traumatic event will develop PTSD. Indeed, most will not. Risk factors include personal or family history of depression or anxiety, severity of the trauma and early separation from parents.

What does PTSD look like?

The symptoms of PTSD develop within 6 months following the traumatic event and are organized into three categories:

Re-experiencing Symptoms – recurrent, intrusive, distressing recollections or memories of the event in the form of memories, dreams, or flashbacks in which the individual perceives himself/herself to be re-living the event as though it was actually happening again in the present.

Avoidance & Numbing Symptoms – avoidance of anything – people, places, topics of conversation, food, drink, weather conditions, clothing, activities, situations, thoughts, feelings – that are associated with or are reminders of the traumatic event. In addition the person may experience a general numbing of emotions, a loss of interest in previously enjoyed activities, detachment from family and friends, and a sense of hopelessness about the future.

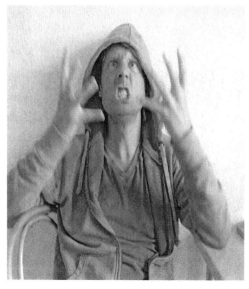

Hyperarousal Symptoms – sleep problems (difficulties falling asleep or staying asleep), irritability, angry outbursts, hypervigilance, exaggerated startle response, and difficulty concentrating.

What are the criteria for the diagnosis of PTSD?

1. The person has been exposed to a traumatic event in which both of the following were present:
    a. The person felt their life was in danger or witnessed someone else's life put in danger
    b. The person experienced extreme fear, helplessness or horror
2. The traumatic event is re-experienced, including one or more of:
    a. Recurrent intrusive memories, dreams or nightmares reliving the event which causes psychological distress.
3. Avoidance of things associated with the event including 3 or more of:
    a. Avoid thoughts, feelings or conversations, avoid activities, places or people, inability to recall aspect of the trauma, decreased interest or participation in activities, feeling detached or estranged from others, restricted range of affect, sense of foreshortened future.
4. Persistent symptoms of increased arousal including 2 or more of:
    a. Difficulty falling or staying asleep, irritability, difficulty concentrating, hypervigilance, exaggerated startle response
5. Duration of symptoms greater than 1 month.

Severity of symptoms causes marked distress and impairment in daily functioning.

How does PTSD differ from Acute Stress Disorder or normal grieving?

PTSD must be distinguished from normal responses (such as grief, distress) to such situations and from Acute Stress Disorder (ASD) which has similar symptoms to PTSD but which ends or diminished greatly usually without formal treatment within four weeks of the traumatic event. Duration and severity of PTDS symptoms may vary over time with complete recovery occurring within half a year or less in half or more cases.

What can I do if it is PTSD?

The first thing is to identify the young person with PTSD and help them find a knowledgeable helper who can provide education to them about what the problem is and how it can be treated. It is important not to confuse PTSD with normal responses to traumatic events or with ASD. Do not create pathology where it does not exist! For people with PTSD, supportive counseling using cognitive therapy methods may be of help. If the disorder is causing significant distress and impairment, referral to an appropriate health care provider is indicated, as medication may be needed.

Things to look for:

Some people who are exposed to significant traumatic events may have exacerbations of pre-existing mental health problems such as anxiety, depression or psychosis. Identification and proper effective interventions for these people in the post traumatic situation is important. Substance abuse, especially involving alcohol is very common in people who have PTSD. Therefore it is important to screen for this problem in people with PTSD and to treat appropriately.

What questions can I ask?

Are you bothered by memories or thoughts of a very upsetting event that has happened to you? Make sure that you ask about frequency and persistence of symptoms and include clear evidence of functional impairment before considering PTSD.

Mental Disorder of Physical: (Eating disorders)

WHAT IS AN EATING DISORDER?

There are two main types of eating disorders – anorexia nervosa and bulimia nervosa. While there may be some overlapping in symptoms between the two, they are likely to have different causes and the treatments for them differ.

Who is at risk for developing an eating disorder?

Eating disorders usually begin in adolescence and may continue into adulthood. Girls are much more commonly affected than boys.

What does Anorexia Nervosa look like?

Anorexia Nervosa (AN) is characterized by excessive preoccupation with body weight control, a disturbed body image, an intense fear of gaining weight and a refusal to maintain a minimally normal weight. Post pubertal girls also experience a loss of menstrual periods. There are two subtypes of AN – a restricting subtype (in which the young person does not regularly binge or abuse laxative or self induce vomiting) and a binge-eating/purging subtype (in which the young person regularly binges and abuses laxatives or self-induces vomiting).

What does Bulimia Nervosa look like?

Bulimia Nervosa (BN) is characterized by regular and recurrent binge eating (large amounts of food over a short time accompanied by a lack of control over the eating during the episode) and by frequent and in appropriate behaviors designed to prevent weight gain (including but not limited to: self-induced vomiting; use of laxatives, enemas; excessive exercise).

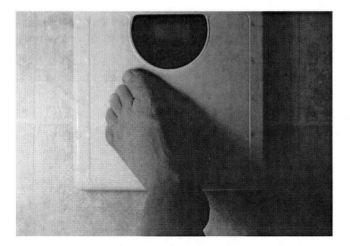

How do you differentiate an eating disorder from normal teenage eating?

Eating patterns in young people can be very erratic. Food fads are common as are periods of dieting and food restriction (often in response to concerns about weight). Adolescence is also a period in which some young people experiment with food types and eating experiments that may differ substantially from those common to their families or communities. These are not eating disorders.

What are the criteria for the diagnosis of AN?

1 – refusal to maintain body weight at or above a minimally normal weight for age and height resulting in a body weight less than 85% of that expected.

2 – intense fear of gaining weight or becoming fat while underweight.

3 – substantial disturbances in body image (considers self to be fat even though is underweight) or denial of seriousness of current low body weight.

4 – loss of menstrual periods in post pubertal girls.

The prevalence of AN is about 0.2 – 0.5 percent.

What can I do if it is AN?

Young people with AN do not complain about having AN and most deny that they have a problem with being underweight. Usually a friend, teacher or family member will notice the severe weight loss. An educator who is concerned that a student may have AN should gently and supportively discuss the issue with the young person and if after that discussion it seems as if there is a possibility of AN the young person should be referred to the appropriate support person or health provider in the school for further assessment and intervention. Suggestions that the young person eat more or negative comments

Things to look for:
Some people with AN may go on to develop a clinical depression. or severe medical problems. Some young people may begin to avoid class or other school activities. Frequently, young people with AN will avoid eating at times all other young people are eating (such as lunch time in the school cafeteria).

on the youth's weight are counterproductive.

What are the criteria for the diagnosis of BN?

1 – recurrent episodes of binge eating where both of the following are present: a) – eating large amounts of food in a short period of time; b) – feeling that eating is out of control.

2 – recurrent inappropriate behaviours in order to control weight (such as: self-induced vomiting; misuse of laxative, diuretics, enemas or other medications, fasting or excessive exercise).

3 – the above must occur an average at least twice a week for a period of 3 months.

4 – self perspective is overly influenced by body shape and weight.

5 – the above does not occur exclusively during AN.

There are two subtypes of BN – the purging type (characterized by self-induced vomiting or misuse of laxative, diuretics, enemas, etc.); the nonpurging type (no use of the above).

The prevalence of BN is about 1 – 3 percent.

What can I do if it is BN?

Young people with BN do not complain about having BN and most deny that they have a problem with eating. BN is often hidden. Classroom discussions about BN and other eating problems should be undertaken with sensitivity that there may be a young person with unknown or unrecognized BN in the group.

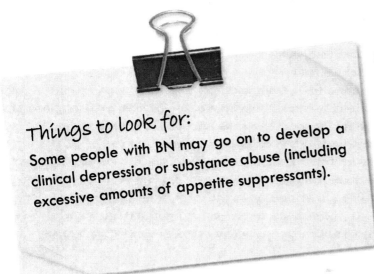

Things to look for:
Some people with BN may go on to develop a clinical depression or substance abuse (including excessive amounts of appetite suppressants).

Questions to ask?

How do you feel about yourself? Has anyone asked you if you were having problems with your eating? Do you sometimes feel that your eating may be out of control?

Mental Disorders of Behaviour: (ADHD, Substance Abuse, Conduct Disorder)

SUBSTANCE DEPENDENCE AND ABUSE

There is a spectrum of harm that can develop from using various substances. Along this spectrum of harm is abuse and dependence.

What is Substance Abuse?

The abuse of substances is a maladaptive pattern of substance use leading to clinically significant impairment or distress, as manifested by one (or more) of the following, occurring within a 12-month period:

1. Recurrent substance use resulting in a failure to fulfill major role obligations at work, school, or home (e.g., repeated absences or poor work performance related to substance use; substance-related absences, suspensions or expulsions from school; neglect of children or household)
2. Recurrent substance use in situations in which it is physically hazardous (e.g., driving an automobile or operating a machine when impaired by substance use)
3. Recurrent substance-related legal problems (e.g., arrests for substance-related disorderly conduct)
4. Continued substance use despite having persistent or

recurrent social or interpersonal problems caused or exacerbated by the effects of the substance (e.g., arguments with spouse about consequences of intoxication, physical fights)

What is Substance Dependence?

Substance dependence is a maladaptive pattern of substance use, leading to clinically significant impairment or distress, as manifested by three (or more) of the following, occurring at any time in the same 12-month period:

1. Tolerance, as defined by either of the following:
   - A need for markedly increased amounts of the substance to achieve intoxication or desired effect.
   - Markedly diminished effect with continued use of the same amount of substance.
2. Withdrawal, as manifested by either of the following:
   - the characteristic withdrawal syndrome for the substance.
   - the same (or a closely related) substance is taken to relieve or avoid withdrawal symptoms.
3. The substance is often taken in larger amounts or over a longer period than was intended.
4. There is a persistent desire or unsuccessful efforts to cut down or control substance use.
5. A great deal of time is spent in activities to obtain the substance, use the substance, or recover from its effects.
6. Important social, occupational or recreational activities are given up or reduced because of substance use.
7. The substance use is continued despite knowledge of having a persistent or recurrent physical or psychological problem that is likely to have been caused or exacerbated by the substance (e.g., continued drinking despite recognition that an ulcer was made worse by alcohol consumption).

What are types of substances that can be abused?

The abuse of substances includes those that are legal and illegal. The definition of a drug as a legal or illegal substance does not determine if the substance can induce dependence or abuse. Substances include such things as alcohol, nicotine, cannabis, amphetamines, cocaine, inhalants, opioids, hypnotics and others.

A variety of substances can be safely used in moderation by most people as social modifiers (for example, beer or other alcohol taken with meals or in social situations). Substances which may be abused in some situations can be therapeutic in others — for example, heroin or cocaine can be used to treat pain under medical supervision but are also well known to be addictive substances when used for non-medical purposes.

What can I do if it is Substance Abuse/Dependence?

First it is important to identify the problem. In some situations, cultural, social or economic factors may impede the identification of the substance problem. The person with the problem will often deny the problem exists and sometimes the person's family or loved ones will also deny that the problem exists. Young people often proceed though a path of substance misuse for a long time (years) before some of them go on to abuse. Most young people who misuse substances likely do not go on to abuse them — therefore substance misuse, although a risk factor for substance abuse is not necessarily predictive of substance abuse. Academic and social problems characterize the young person who suffers from substance abuse — failing grades, missing classes, Monday morning absences, aggression, etc.

Things to look for:

Some people with substance dependence/abuse will also have other mental health problems such as depression or anxiety. If these problems occur they should be identified and help for them provided. Suicide may occur more frequently in people with substance problems. Youth who suffer from untreated or inadequately treated ADHD are at higher risk for substance abuse. Effective medication treatment of ADHD decreases the risk for substance abuse.

Questions to ask?

Try to determine the amounts of the substance used – remember that use can be continuous (for example: daily) or in binge patterns (large amounts used sporadically – such as every three to five days). Determine if the young persons problems are due in whole or in part to excessive use of substances. One particularly important question is – "How does taking (name of substance here) help you or hinder you in your school and social life?"

Substance abuse/dependence in young people usually requires professional intervention. Issues such as confidentiality will often arise so it is important that teachers understand what the expectations and limits to confidentiality regarding substance abuse/dependence are in their setting.

Often the advice of a teacher or coach is an important step towards treatment for a young person abusing substances. Non-judgemental but realistic advice from a teacher can sometimes lead them to the realization that they need help. Some young people traffic in the substances that they use. The teacher therefore needs to know the school policy on drugs and abide by it.

What is attention deficit hyperactivity disorder?

Attention Deficit Hyperactivity Disorder(ADHD) is characterized by a persistent pattern of hyperactivity, impulsivity adn substantial difficulties with sustained attention that is outside the poopulation norm and is associated with substantial functional impairments at school, home and with peers. This disorder begins before age seven and continues into adolescence or for some people, even into adulthood.

Who is at risk for ADHD?

ADHD has a genetic component and runs in many families and is more common in boys than in girls. Girls who have ADHD often do not have similar problems with hyperactivity although they have similar problems with sustaining attention. Young peope who have learning disabilities and youth with Tourette's Syndrome have higher rates of ADHD. Young people with Conduct Disorder may have ADHD which has not been recognized or treated and which may contribute to their social and legal difficulties.

What does ADHD look like?

Problems with sustaining attention may result in substantial difficulties in on task behaviours. Young people with ADHD frequently make multiple careless errors, do not complete their academic or house tasks, may start numerous activities. They are easily distracted by stimuli in their environment (such as noises) and often will begin to avoid tasks that require signficant attention (such as housework). Young people with ADHD will often rush into things such as games or other activities without taking the time to learn the rules or determine what they should do.

Hyperactivity is often menifested by difficulties staying still in one place -- such as sitting at a desk or in a group. Younger children may run around the room or climb on furniture, etc. instead of focusing on group activities. Most young people with ADHD have trouble sitting still and are very active -- often they will fidget, talk excessively, make noises during quiet activitiy and generally seem 'wound up' or 'driven'.

IImpulsivity is often shown as impatience or low frustration tolerance. Young people with ADHD will often interrupt others, fail to listen to instructions, rush into novel situations without thinking about the consequences, etc. This type of behaviour may lead to accidents. Many youth with ADHD also do not seem to be able to learn from negative experiences, it is as if the impulsivity overrides learning about dangers.

These difficulties can be less pronounced in activities that require a great deal of physical particiopation and are constantly engaging. Sometimes young people with ADHD seem less distracted when they are playing games that they like -- especially games that do not require sustained attention (such as video games). Symptoms are more likley to be noticed when the young person is in a group setting in which sustained and quiet attention is needed or when he/she is working in an environment in which there are many distrractions.

What are the criteria for diagnosis of ADHD?

There are must be a number of symptoms from each of the following categories: inattention; hyperactivity; impulsivity PLUS a duration of atleast six months to a defree that the person deomstrates maladaptive behaviours and trouble functioning that is inconsistent with their level of development.

Inattention (atleast six of the following)
1- failure to give close attention or many careless errors in work requiring sustained attention (such as school work)
2 - difficulty sustaining attention in tasks or play
3 - does not seem to listen when spoken to directly
4 - does not follow through on instructions
5 - has difficulty organizing tasks and activities
6 - avoides tasks that require sustained attention (such as homework)
7 - lose things needed for tasks and activities
8 - easily distracted by the environment
9 - forgotful in daily activities

Hyperactivity

1 - fidgets or squirms while seated
2 - leaves eeat in classroom or when is suppose to be seated
3 - runs about or climbs excessively when not appropriate
4 - has difficulty in soliatry play or quiet activities
5 - is usually on the go, as if motor driven
6 - often talks excessively

Impulsivity (are included in the number of symptoms for hyperactivity)
7 - blurts out comments or answers to questions before he/she should
8 - has difficulty waiting for his/her turn
9 - often interrupts or intrudes on others

What can I do if it is ADHD?

ADHD can be treated with a combincation of medications and other assistance -- such as social skills training and cognitive behavioural therapy. The most effective treatment for symptoms is medication. Because learning difficulties are common, young people with ADHD should undergo educational testing to determine if their learning disability is present. Sometimes youth with ADHD will benefit from modifications to their learning environments such as having quieter places in which to work or having homework done in small amounts over long periods of time.

Some young people with ADHD will develop conduct disturbances or substances abuse. Many will become demoralized because of constant reminders from teachers, parents and others about their 'bad behaviour'. Remember that these young people are not bad - they simply have difficulties with sustained attention. Try not to decrease their self-esteem by focusing only on what they have difficulty doing - focus on their strengths as well.

Questions to ask?

Are you having difficulties focusing on your schoolwork? Is it hard for you to finish your work if there are noises or distractions? Do your parents or teachers seem to be nagging you all the time to do your work and sit still?

Things to look for:

Some young people with ADHD will develop conduct distrubances or substance abuse. Many will become demoralized because of constant reminders from teachers, parents and others about their 'bad behavour'. Remember that these young people are not bad -- they simply have difficulties with sustained attention. Try not to decrease their self-esteem by focusing only on what they have difficulty doing- focus on strengths as well.

What is suicide?

Suicide the act of ending one's life. Suicide itself is not a mental disorder but one of the most important causes of suicide is mental illness – most often depression, bipolar disorder (manic depression), schizophrenia, and substance abuse.

Suicide is found in every culture and may be the result of complex social, cultural, religious and socio-economic factors in addition to mental disorders. The reasons for suicide may vary from region to region because of these factors. It is therefore important to know what the most common reasons for suicide are in the region in which you are working. This may be difficult to determine accurately because of the "taboos" and stigma around suicide.

The preferred methods of completing suicide may vary from location to location – ranging from firearms to fertilizer poisoning to self-burning to overdosing on pills. Therefore, it is also important to know the most common methods of suicide in the region in which you are working.

What does suicide look like?

Not all self-harm behaviors are attempts to commit suicide. There may be many reasons for self-harm behaviors besides suicide. These include a person attempting to cry for help, for example from a person who is stuck in a harmful situation that they cannot escape such as ongoing sexual abuse. Certain types of personality disorders commonly perform self-harm behaviors. A suicide attempt is distinguished from a self-harm behavior by the person's intent to die.

Suicidal behavior has three components: ideation; intent, plans.

1. Suicidal ideation includes ideas about death or dying, wishing that he/she were dead, or ideas about committing suicide. These ideas are not persistent. These ideas can be fairly common in people with mental disorders or in people who are in difficult life circumstances. Most people with suicidal ideation do not go on to commit suicide but the suicidal ideation is a risk factor for suicide.
2. The second component is suicidal intent. With suicidal intent, the idea of committing suicide is better formed and more consistently held than in suicidal ideation. A person with suicidal intent may think about committing suicide most of the time, imaging what life would be like for friends and family without him/her, etc. The strongest intent occurs when the person decides that she/he will commit suicide.
3. The third component is the suicide plan. This is a clear plan of how the act of suicide will occur. Vague plans (such as "someday I will jump off a bridge") are considered as part of intent. In a suicide plan the means of committing suicide will be identified and obtained (such a gun, poison, etc.), the place and time will be chosen. The presence of a suicide plan constitutes a psychiatric emergency.

What can I do if it is Suicide?

The first thing is to identify the presence of suicide ideation, intent and plans. Suicide ideation and intent may benefit from supportive or cognitive based counseling. The presence of a suicide plan should lead to placement of the person in a situation in which he/she can be safe and secure. That situation should be therapeutic and not punitive and should be accompanied by supportive and cognitive counseling. The family or loved ones may require support and help as well. Non-judgmental supportive counseling may be of assistance in such situation. If a suicide has happened, the family or loved ones may benefit from non-judgmental supportive bereavement counseling.

If a teacher is faced with a student who is talking about or writing about suicide then it is important to include an educator from guidance or health to assess the situation. Generally it is better to err on the side of caution and take the young person to a location in which they can be safe. Schools should have policies about how to deal with a suicidal youth – know your school's policy. If there is no policy bring this issue to the attention of the principal.

If a young person suicides, there can be negative repercussions amongst peers, classmates and teachers. It is important not to force students or others into reliving or analyzing the event. Traditional critical incident stress debriefing interventions have not been shown to be helpful and may even cause harm. A supportive space for those students who wish to use it should be provided after school hours and a teacher or guidance counselor known to the students should ideally be available for those who wish to talk. Each community will have its own traditions for dealing with this kind of event and it is not necessary to create highly affective responses to a suicide in the school setting.

What are risk factors for suicide?

The following are the most common (and strongest) risk factors for suicide in young people. Remember that a risk factor does not mean something that causes an event to happen, rather it is something that is related to an event that happens.

- Sex (male)
- Depression or other mental disorder
- Previous suicide attempt
- Family history of suicide
- Excessive alcohol or drug use
- Impulsivity or juvenile justice history

Suicide risk is high in people with mental disorders, in particular those with: depression (of all kinds); bipolar (manic-depression); schizophrenia; substance abuse. If a young person talks to you about suicide, take them seriously – it is a myth that people who talk about suicide will not attempt suicide.

Questions to ask?

Ask about ideation: "Have you been thinking about dying, harming yourself or suicide?"
Ask about intent: "Have you decided that you would be better off dead or that you should kill yourself?"
Ask about plans: "What plans have you made to kill yourself (and obtain the details)?"

What should I do:

1. If you suspect that a young person may have a mental disorder, it is necessary to refer them to the designated mental health professional (guidance counselor, psychologist, social worker) in the school.
2. If you suspect that a young person may be suicidal, immediately contacting your school designated emergency coordinator or principal is necessary.

Tell students that their responses to these questions will not be graded, and that the questions do not have a single "correct" answer. These open-ended questions give students a chance to express what they already know about mental health and mental illness before experiencing any of the materials in the curriculum guide. Many students, as well as many adults, carry misconceptions about mental illness, and this activity will draw their conceptions to the surface.

Activity 1:

Purpose:

- To have students reflect on their understanding and attitudes toward mental health and mental illness

- To provide a baseline snapshot of students' ideas of mental illness that can be reexamined at the end of the modules taught so that students and teachers can see the impact of the material on their learning

How to:

1) Give each student a copy of the "What do you think?" questionnaire. Ask students to take 10 minutes on their own to complete the questionnaire.

2) Ask students to fold their completed copies of the questionnaire in half. Have them write their names on the outside and staple the papers closed.

   At this time, do not provide answers or make judgments about students' responses inform them that no one will look at their answers until they do so themselves at the end of the module.

3) Collect the students' papers and save them until after all modules have been taught.

Questionnaire: What do you think?

Today's date:_____ Birthdate: _____ Gender: ____

Write two or three sentences to answer each of the following questions:

1) What is mental health?

2) What is mental illness?

3) Name some mental illnesses that you have heard about.

4) How would a person with mental illness look or act?

5) If you learned that a new student at school has a mental illness, how would you act toward him or her? How would you feel about him or her?

6) What causes someone to be mentally ill?

Adapted from *The Science of Mental Illness*, http://science.education.nih.gov/supplements/mental

At least some of the student's answers should be different now that they have learned more about mental illness. Even if some students' attitudes have not changed within the span of this unit, the knowledge they have gained may influence their opinions about how people who have a mental illness should be treated.

Notice that the discussion questions above do not ask students to divulge their answers. Because of the potentially sensitive nature of the questions, students may be uncomfortable sharing what they wrote. Use your judgment in discussing responses to specific questions. The discussion will need to be handled with sensitivity because students may bring up personal experiences or stories. You might want to ask the school guidance counselor or other support staff to be present, or to help facilitate the discussion.

Activity 2: (15 mins.)

What do you think about mental illness now?*

Purpose:
- To provide students with an opportunity to reflect on the changes in their knowledge and attitudes about mental illness from the first module.

How to:

1) Hand out a copy of the "What do you think" questionnaire to each student and have them answer the questions.

2) After students have answered the questions, give each student their copy of the questionnaire that they completed in Module 2. Ask students to compare the answers they just wrote with the answers they wrote in the earlier module. Give students a few minutes to compare their responses, reminding them that they should only be looking at their own answers. Ask students whether their answers are different today, and if so, how they are different.

3) Conduct a brief group discussion around students' responses. Use the following questions as a guide:

- If your answers were different today, why do you think they were different?

- Does learning about mental illness make a difference? Why?

- Do you think you would react differently now to someone who has mental illness compared to your reaction before you completed this unit?

4) Consider compiling the students' responses and submitting them to CMHA National office for evaluation purposes.

CMHA
595 Montreal Road, Suite 303
Ottawa, ON K1K 4C2

tel: (613) 745-7750
fax: (613) 745-5522

Questionnaire: What do you think?

Today's date: _____   Birthdate: _____   Gender: _____

Write two or three sentences to answer each of the following questions:

1) What is mental health?

2) What is mental illness?

3) Name some mental illnesses that you have heard about.

4) How would a person with mental illness look or act?

5) If you learned that a new student at school has a mental illness, how would you act toward him or her? How would you feel about him or her?

6) What causes someone to be mentally ill?

*Adapted from *The Science of Mental Illness,* http://science.education.nih.gov/supplements/mental

MODULES

Part 4

Module 1: The stigma of mental illness

Module 2: Understanding mental health and mental illness

Module 3: Information on specific mental illness

Module 4: Experiences of mental illness

Module 5: Seeking help and finding support

Module 6: The importance of positive mental health

The stigma of mental illness

Overview

Many people with mental illness say that the stigma that surrounds mental illness is harder to live with than the disease itself.

In the context of the curriculum guide, stigma refers to "a cluster of negative attitudes and beliefs that motivate the general public to fear, reject, avoid and discriminate against people with mental illness. Stigma is not just a matter of using the wrong word or action. Stigma is about disrespect. It is the use of negative labels to identify a person living with mental illness. Stigma is a barrier. Fear of stigma and the resulting discrimination discourages individuals and their families from getting the help they need." (SAMHSA, 2004)

In the United States, the Surgeon General's Report on Mental Health (1999) cites studies showing that nearly two-thirds of all people with diagnosable mental disorders do not seek treatment (Regier et al. , 1993; Kessler et al., 1996). While the reasons for this are varied, we know that stigma surrounding the receipt of mental health services is a significant barrier that discourages people from seeking treatment, and that stigma may be intensifying instead of abating over time (Sussman et al., Cooper-Patrick et al., 1997).

The activities in this section will explore the nature of stigma, its impact on the lives of people with mental illness, and effective ways of combating stigma.

Learning objectives

In this module students will:

- Understand the stigma surrounding mental health problems, and the impact of stigma and discrimination on help-seeking behaviour
- Explore the differences between the myths and realities of mental illness
- Investigate the attitudes of people in the school community about mental illness
- Learn ways of overcoming stigma and promoting a realistic and positive understanding of mental illness

Major concepts addressed

- Stigma results in discriminatory behaviour and treatment towards people with mental illness
- The fear of stigma prevents people from seeking help and treatment for mental illness
- Stigma is perpetuated through mistaken beliefs about mental illness, and can be seen in people's attitudes, in public policy, in the media, etc.

Major concepts addressed (cont.)

- Stigma and discrimination can be reduced by providing accurate information about mental illness and its treatment

Teacher background and preparation:

Read through the activities and preview video component before class. To prepare for Module 1, students need to survey five to ten people about their attitudes toward mental health problems and people with mental illness.

How to:

Hand out a copy of the Community Attitudes survey and request that students survey a minimum of five and a maximum of ten people from the school, their household or the broader community. Remind students to bring their results in for the lesson.

Note to teachers:

Discuss with students the sensitive nature of the questionnaire and warn them that some people they approach might not want to answer it.

In advance:

- Make photocopies of Activity Handouts one per student
- Set up web-based video component of Video Section 1: Living with Stigma

The support materials are located on:
http://teenmentalhealth.org/curriculum/support-materials/

The username is: **resource_user**
The password is: **t33nh3alth**

Activities

- Activity 1: Defining stigma

- Activity 2: Exploring attitudes - survey

- Activity 3: Video - Courageous not Crazy Part 1: Living with Stigma

- Activity 4: Reducing Stigma - What works?

MODULE 1

Materials Required

Handouts for Activities 1, 2 and 4
Courageous Not Crazy video Part 1: *Living with Stigma*

Note to teachers:

Our society often attaches a variety of labels to mental illness - psycho, nuts, crazy, wacko and so on. These terms reinforce the stigma associated with mental illness. In the class-room, it's more appropriated to use the term "person with mental illness".

The following is some general information about Canadian community attitudes towards mental illness and effective ways of addressing mental health problems. You can use this informantion to compare and contrast with students findings.

According to a 2007 Report on Mental Health Literacy in Canada prepared by the Canadian Alliance on Mental Health and Mental Illness, most Canadians:

- Have difficulty recognizing and correctly identifying mental disorders
- Prefer psychosocial explanations for mental disorders over biomedical ones, e.g. prefer to think that depression is caused by stress then a chemical imbalance or other prob-lems that are happening in the brain
- Do not know how to deal with people with mental disorders
- Do not consider common mental health problems (anxiety/mild to moderate depression) as mental illnesses, and have relatively benign attitudes towards these disorders
- Associate mental illness with psychotic disorders and are fearful of those labeled "men-tally ill"
- Are often reluctant to seek professional help
- Have negative attitudes towards psychiatric medications
- Are often reluctant to disclose mental disorders for fear of stigma and discrimination

Additionally:

- A significant minority of Canadians hold stigmatizing attitudes towards mental illness, and many believe that others subscribe to these views
- Serious mental illness, especially psychosis, is more feared and stigmatized than com-mon mental health problems
- People remain concerned about disclosing common mental health problems, particular-ily in the workplace, for fear of discrimination

V

Our society often attaches a variety of labels to mental illness which act to reinforce stigma. In the classroom it's more appropriate to use the term "person with mental illness".

Remind students that everyone has some stigmatizing or discriminatory thoughts or attitudes, and that the key message here is that we need to recognize those stigmatizing or discriminatory thoughts or attitudes, examine where they come from, and work toward changing the hurtful behaviours they cause.

Activity 1: (10 mins.)
Defining stigma*

Purpose:

*   To explore the meaning of the term stigma and the relationship between attitudes (beliefs) and discriminatory treatment (behaviour and actions) toward people with mental illness.

How to:

1) Ask students if they know what the word "stigma" means. Lead a whole-class discussion of the definition of stigma, and the relationship between stigma, stereotyping and discrimination.

Questions to guide discussion:

*   What are some of the negative things you have heard about people with mental illness? (responses may include things like: link to violence, etc)
*   What are some of the positive things you have heard about mental illness? (Responses may include things like: link to creativity). While this may be seen as positive, remind students that generalizing can also be a form of stereotyping.
*   Why do you think people with mental illness are stigmatized? (possible answers include: They are seen as being different. People don't really know the facts about mental illness)
*   Can you think of any other health conditions or social issues that have been stigmatized throughout history? (possible answers include: homosexuality, leprosy, AIDS, unwed motherhood, divorce)
*   What kinds of factors have contributed to changing public attitudes around some of these conditions or issues? (possible answers include: education, public policy, open dialogue, scientific research, changing social mores)
*   What do you think influences perceptions about mental illness? (possible answers include: the media – films, news, newspaper headlines and stories that associate people with mental illness with violence, the fact that people with mental illness sometimes behave differently and people are afraid of what they don't understand)
*   How do you think stigma affects the lives of people with mental illness? (possible answers include: people decide not to get help and treatment even though they would benefit from it, it makes them unhappy, they may not be able to get a job or find housing, it may cause them to lose their friends, it puts stress on the whole family)

*This activity has been adapted from *Talking About Mental Illness*, CAMH 2001
http://www.camh.net/education/Resources_teachers_schools/TAMI/tami_teachersall.pdf

Defining stigma

The following are definitions of "stigma" taken from different sources and from different historical periods

> A mark or sign of disgrace or discredit; a visible sign or characteristic of disease.
> *- The Concise Oxford Dictionary, 1990*
>
> An attribute which is deeply discrediting.
> *- Goffman, E. Stigma: The management of Spoiled Identity. 1963*
>
> A distinguishing mark or characteristic of a bad or objectionable kind; a sign of some specific disorder, as hysteria; a mark made upon the skin by burning with a hot iron, as a token of infamy or subjection; a brand; a mark of disgrace or infamy; a sign of severe censure or condemnation, regarded as impressed on a person or thing."
> *- The Shorter Oxford Dictionary, Fourth Edition, 1993*

The stigma of mental illness

"Stigma refers to a cluster of negative attitudes and beliefs that motivate the general public to fear, reject, avoid and discriminate against people with mental illnesses. Stigma is not just a matter of using the wrong word or action. Stigma is about disrespect. It is the use of negative labels to identify a person living with mental illness. Stigma is a barrier. Fear of stigma and the resulting discrimination discourages individuals and their families from getting the help they need." *(SAMHSA 2004)*

Terms related to Stigma

Stereotype:
"a person or thing that conforms to an unjustly fixed impression or attitude"
Stereotypes are the attitudes about a group of people, e.g.
"All people with mental illness are dangerous."

Prejudice:
"A preconceived opinion"
Prejudice is agreeing with the stereotypes, e.g.
"I think people with mental illness are dangerous."

Discrimination:
"unfavourable treatment based on prejudice"
Discrimination is the behavior that results: "I don't want people with mental illness around me, therefore I discriminate against them by not hiring them, not being friends with them, etc."
- The Concise Oxford Dictionary, 1990

(* This activity has been adapted from "Talking About Mental Illness, CAMH 2001)

MODULE 1

Activity 2: (20 mins.)
Examining Community Attitudes - Analyzing survey results*

Purpose:

- To collate the results of the survey completed by students and examine and analyze the results with the class
- To compare their results with the Community Attitudes Survey: Best Answers and draw conclusions about the community's awareness of mental health and illness in relation to broader Canadian attitudes

How to:

1) In groups of four or five, students share survey responses to get a better picture of the attitudes of the larger sample. If time permits (or as a possible follow up project for those who are interested), students could use the computer to collate and graph the survey results.

2) Ask students to come up with some general conclusions from the grouped survey findings to share with the rest of the class, for example:
   - Our sample was not well informed about mental illnesses because X % responded...

   - The women in our sample were more tolerant about mental illness than the men

   - Only half the people surveyed agreed that they would have someone with a mental illness as a close friend

3) Facilitate a class-wide discussion about the survey results, highlighting ways in which the results inform us about peoples' attitudes about mental illness. Refer to the Community Attitudes Survey: Best Answers, to ground the discussion and answer any questions that students might have. Use the sample questions below as a guide for discussion.

Sample Questions:

- What do the responses tell you about the level of awareness about mental illness in the community?
- What role do you think the media plays in shaping peoples' attitudes?
- Do you think your results reflect the Canadian community attitudes more generally? Why or why not?
- Do you think it's possible to change community attitudes toward mental illness?
- How might this be done?

---

*adapted from *MindMatters: Understanding Mental Illness*, pg. 57.

MODULE 1

Community Attitudes Survey

Check the most appropriate answer:	Agree	Disagree	Not sure
1) People should work out their own mental health problems			
2) Once you have a mental illness, you have it for life			
3) Females are more likely to have a mental illness then males			
4) Medication is the best treatment for mental illness			
5) People with a mental illness are generally violent and dangerous			
6) Adults are more likely than teenagers to have a mental illness			
7) You can by looking at someone whether they have a mental illness			
8) People with a mental illness are generally shy and quiet			
9) Mental illness can happen to anybody			
10) You would be willing to have a person with a mental illness at your school or at your work			
11) You would be happy to have a person with mental illness become a close friend			

Respondent	M/F	Under 19	20-29	30-39	40-49	50 and up
#1						
#2						
#3						
#4						
#5						
#6						
#7						
#8						
#9						
#10						

*Adapted from *Mind Matters: Understanding Mental Illness*, pg 57

Community Attitudes Survey: Best Answers

1) People should work out their own mental health problems.

Not true. When people have a physical health concern, they generally take some action, and often go to the doctor or seek some other kind of help for their problem. Mental illness is associated with disturbances with brain functioning and usually requires professional assistance. Because of the stigma surrounding mental illness, many people have been reluctant to seek help.

2) Once you have a mental illness, you have it for life.

While it's true that most mental illnesses are lifelong, they are often episodic, which means that the symptoms are not always present. Just like people who live with chronic physical illnesses like arthritis and asthma, people with mental illnesses can, when their illness is managed, live positive and productive lives.

3) Females are more likely to have a mental illness then males.

Men and women are both equally affected by mental illnesses in general, but there may be higher rates among women of specific illnesses such as eating disorders.
There may sometimes be higher rates in women for other disorders such as depression. Men have higher rates for some disorders such as alcoholism and ADHD. Some illnesses are relatively equally shared by both men and women (e.g. bipolar disorder).

Women are more likely to seek help for mental and emotional difficulties and to share their concerns with friends compared to men. Females are more willing to let friends know if they are receiving counselling. In practice, 62% of women would probably or definitely want their friends to know compared to 45% of men.

(Canadian Mental Health Survey COMPAS Inc.
Multi-Audience Research Ottawa and Toronto April 20, 2001)
http://www.cmha.ca/bins/content_page.asp?cid=5-34-212-213#_
Toc512618127

4) Medication is the best treatment for mental illness

Medication can be a very effective part of managing a mental illness, but it is by no means the only type of treatment or support that helps people recover. A wide range of appropriate interventions, including medication, counselling, social, vocational and housing-related supports, as well as self-help and generic resources for all community members (such as: groups, clubs, and religious institutions) are also important in helping people recover and stay well.

It is helpful to think of medications as necessary but not sufficient treatments for many mental disorders. The best approach is to have a combination of strategies that have been proven effective.

5) People with a mental illness are generally violent and dangerous.

People with mental illness are generally not more violent than the rest of the population. Mental illness plays no part in the majority of violent crimes committed in our society. The assumption that any and every mental illness carries with it an almost certain potential for violence has been proven wrong in many studies.

6) Adults are more likely than teenagers to have a mental illness.

Many of the major mental illnesses begin to appear during adolescence and early adulthood.

7) You can by looking at someone whether they have a mental illness.

Generally, you can't tell if a person has a mental illness based on their appearance. Sometimes, when people are experiencing an acute episode of their illness, their behaviour may be bizarre, especially if they are experiencing an episode of psychosis.

Community Attitudes Survey: Best Answers

8) People with a mental illness are generally shy and quiet.

There is no strong causal relationship between personality characteristics and tendency to develop mental illness. Some mental disorders such as depression and anxiety can lead people to avoid or limit social contact.

9) Mental illness can happen to anybody.

This is correct. In fact, it very likely that you, a family member or someone you're close to will experience a mental illness at some point in their lives.

10) You would be willing to have a person with a mental illness at your school or at your work

11) You would be happy to have a person with mental illness become a close friend

Questions 10 and 11 both address the issue of "social distance", that is, the willingness to engage in relationships of varying intimacy with a person. Social distance is an indicator of public attitudes toward people with mental illness.

Social distance is a complex concept influenced by a number of factors, including age, gender, socio-economic and cultural factors, but also by the respondent's general attitude toward mental health issues.

Contact, or social inclusion of people with mental illness with the rest of the population, is the factor that usually that leads to a decrease in stigma. This aids in bringing about significant changes in attitudes and behavior that are maintained over time. This can happen when people find out that a coworker, neighbour or friend is struggling with mental illness, and despite it, is living on their own, working and being a part of the community.

(Adapted from Mind Matters: Understanding Mental Illness, pg. 57)*

MODULE 1

Video – Courageous Not Crazy: Living with stigma

Purpose:

- To provide students with an opportunity to learn about the impact of stigma on young people's lives
- To help students develop an understanding of the living with stigma – the social consequences that are a part of living with a mental illness.

How-to:

1) Set up online video to show the class as a whole or arrange small groups at computers to view Courageous Not Crazy Part 1: Living with Stigma to watch.

The support materials are located on:
http://teenmentalhealth.org/curriculum/support-materials/

The username is: **resource_user**
The password is: **t33nh3alth**

This section of the video addresses the experience of living with the stigma of mental illness, and how stigma has impacted on the lives of the young people interviewed.

2) At the end of the video, lead a brief discussion of students' impressions of the video, and distribute photocopies of Activity 4 Handout Reducing Stigma: What works?

MODULE 1

Handout: Reducing Stigma - What Works?

Purpose:

- To provide students with ideas about what they can do to reduce the stigma of mental illness in their everyday lives

How-to:

1) Distribute the handouts and encourage students to apply the strategies for reducing stigma in the school, at home, and in the community.

2) Remind students that things have improved since the days of the "looney bin"; however, there are still many examples of how people living with mental illness are portrayed as violent as well as ridiculed in the media and popular culture. Have students think about topical stories from the news and/or movies and TV shows.

Reducing Stigma – What Works?

There is no simple or single strategy to eliminate the stigma associated with mental illness, but some positive steps can be taken. Research is showing that negative perceptions about severe mental illness can be changed by:

- **Providing information based on reliable research** that refutes the mistaken association between violence and severe mental illness *(Penn & Martin, 1998)*.

- **Effective advocacy and public education programs** can help to shift attitudes and contribute to the reduction of stigma *(Surgeon General Report on Mental Health, 1999)*.

- **Proximity or direct contact with people with mental illness** tends to reduce negative stereotypes *(Corrigan & Penn, 1999)*.

- **Programs that help people to become better integrated in the community** through school, work, integrated housing, or interest-based social groups not only serve to promote the individual's mental health by reducing exclusion, but also can play a part in gradually shifting commonly-held negative attitudes.

- **Treatments and supports** that work to help people recover.

Reducing Stigma – What works? (cont.)

LEARN MORE ABOUT MENTAL ILLNESS
If you are well-informed about mental illness, you will be better able to evaluate and resist the inaccurate negative stereotypes that you come across.

LISTEN TO PEOPLE WHO HAVE EXPERIENCED MENTAL ILLNESS
These individuals can describe what they find stigmatizing, how stigma affects their lives and how they would like to be viewed and treated.

WATCH YOUR LANGUAGE
Most of us, even mental health professionals and people who have mental illness, use terms and expressions related to mental illness that may perpetuate stigma.

RESPOND TO STIGMATIZING MATERIAL IN THE MEDIA
Keep your eyes peeled for media that stigmatizes mental illness and report it to any number of organizations. Get in touch with the people--authors, editors, movie producers, advertisers--responsible for the material. Write, call or email them yourself, expressing your concerns and providing more accurate information that they can use.

SPEAK UP ABOUT STIGMA
When someone you know misuses a psychiatric term (such as schizophrenia), let them know and educate them about the correct meaning. When someone says something negative about a person with mental illness, tells a joke that ridicules mental illness, or makes disrespectful comments about mental illness, let them know that it is hurtful and that you find such comments offensive and unacceptable.

TALK OPENLY ABOUT MENTAL ILLNESS
Don't be afraid to let others know of your mental illness
or the mental illness of a loved one.
The more mental illness remains hidden, the more people continue to believe that it is a shameful thing that needs
to be kept hidden.

DEMAND CHANGE FROM YOUR ELECTED REPRESENTATIVES
Policies that perpetuate stigma can be changed if enough people let their elected representatives, like city councilors, members of Provincial and Federal Parliament know that
they want such change.

PROVIDE SUPPORT FOR ORGANIZATIONS THAT FIGHT STIGMA
Join, volunteer, donate money. The influence and effectiveness of organizations fighting the stigma surrounding mental illness depend to a large extent on the efforts of volunteers and on donations. You can make a contribution by getting involved.

Adapted from: *Telling is Risky Business: Mental Health Consumers Confront Stigma*. By: Otto Wahl (Rutgers University Press)

MODULE 2

Preparation

Understanding Mental Health and Mental Illness

Overview

Many young people do not know basic facts about mental health and mental illness. In fact, many people confuse the terms: mental health and mental illness. Before thinking about the problems that occur in the brain when someone has a mental illness, it is helpful to think about how the brain functions normally.

In this module, students will be introduced to the basics of brain function, and will learn that the brain processes and reacts to everything we experience. Its activities initiate and control movement, thinking, perception, involuntary physiological processes, as well as emotions. Students will learn that the brain function determines both mental health and mental illness, and that the two are not mutually exclusive.

Learning objectives

In this lesson students will learn:

- Some of the basic concepts involved in normal brain function, and the role the brain plays in determining our thoughts, feelings and behaviours

- That mental health and mental illness both include a wide range of states

- That having a mental health problem is not the same thing as having a mental illness

- Some of the language of mental health and mental illness

Major concepts addressed

- Everyone has mental health regardless of whether or not they have mental illness

- The brain is responsible for our thoughts, actions and behaviours

- Changes in brain function cause changes in thoughts, feelings and behavoiurs that can last a short or long time

- A mental illness affects a person's thinking, feelings or behaviour (or all three) and that causes that person distress and difficulty in functioning

- Mental illnesses have complex causes including a biological basis and are therefore not that different from other illnesses or diseases. As with all serious illnesses, the sooner people get help and treatment for mental illness, the better their long and short-term outcomes

- Many of the major mental illnesses begin to emerge during adolescence

Activities

- Activity 1: Language Brainstorm (20 mins.)

- Activity 2: PowerPoint presentation: (25 mins.)
  Mental Health and Mental Illness: The Common Basis

Teacher background:
- Read through the activities and definitions provided
- Preview Part 1 of the PowerPoint Presentation:
  Mental Health and Mental Illness : The Common Basis

In advance:
Set up computers or projector to show PowerPoint presentation
- Photocopy handouts for Activity 1, one for each student

Materials required:
- Handout Activity 1 Definitions.
- Flip chart paper, markers and tape

V

It's important to emphasize that there are no wrong answers in a brainstorm. This exercise is all about opening up a discussion. Tell students that don't have to agree with or believe in the ideas or names they offer.

Activity 1:   (20 mins.)

Language Brainstorm˙

Purpose:

* To provide an icebreaker that encourages students to participate in an open discussion about a topic not often addressed in the classroom

* To get an idea of students' knowledge about mental health and illness and what their fears and misconceptions might be

* To highlight the ways we tend to conceptualize mental illness

* To set the stage for introducing information on mental health and mental illness in the next activity

How to:

1) Divide the class into 4 groups.

2) Give each group a piece of flip chart paper with one of four terms written at the top: Physical health / Mental health / Physical illness / Mental illness.

3) Give the groups five minutes to brainstorm all the words that come to mind when they see their term.

4) After five minutes, ask groups to tape their sheets up on a wall for all groups to see.

5) Ask one student from each group to read out their list for the whole class.

6) Ask students what they notice about the type of words used on each sheet.

7) Discuss the similarities and differences in student responses to mental and physical aspects of people's health.

8) Ask students to suggest some reasons for these differences.

9) Give students handout of definitions of mental health and mental illness and lead a brief discussion on the definitions.

Definitions

Mental Health

"Mental health is the emotional and spiritual resilience that enables us to enjoy life and survive pain, disappointment, and sadness. It is a positive sense of well-being and an underlying belief in our own and other's self worth." *(Health Education Authority, UK, 1997)*

Who's Got Mental Health?

Everyone – we all have mental health just like we all have physical health. People with mental illness also have mental health, just as people with a physical illness also have physical well-being.

Mental Illness

Mental illness is a term that describes a variety of psychiatric (emotional , thinking and behavioral) problems that vary in intensity and duration, and may recur from time to time. Major mental illnesses include Anxiety, Mood, Eating, and Psychotic disorders. Mental illnesses are diagnosable conditions that require medical treatment as well as other supports. *(www.cmha.ca)*

Mental Health Problems

Mental health problems refer to the more common struggles and adjustment difficulties that affect everybody from time-to-time. These problems tend to happen when people are going through difficult times in life, such as a relationship ending, the death of someone close, conflict in relations with family or friends, or stresses at home, school or work. Feeling stressed or having the blues is a normal response to the psychological or social challenges most people encounter at some time or another. Mental health problems are usually short-term reactions to a particular stressor, such as a loss, painful event, or illness. *(Mental Illness Foundation, 2003)*.

MODULE 2

PowerPoint presentation -
Mental Health and Mental Illness: The Common Basis

Purpose:

- To provide an introduction to basic brain functioning for students to help them understand that the brain controls our thoughts, feelings and behaviours
- To illustrate that mental health and mental illness are related to each other, but that they are not mutually exclusive
- To show that some changes in brain function cause changes in thoughts, feelings and behaviour that last a short or a long time.

How to:

- Use the web version of the presentation by logging on to:

    http://teenmentalhealth.org/curriculum/support-materials/

    The username is: **resource_user**
    The password is: **t33nh3alth**

    see Module 2/Activity 2: Mental Health and Mental Illness: The Common Basis.

- Play the presentation, pausing if needed.

MODULE 3

Information on specific mental illnesses

Overview

In this module, students will learn more about the most common forms of mental illness, paying special attention to those that generally affect adolescents.

Learning objectives

In this module, students will

- Recognize that mental illnesses are associated with differences in brain activity
- Gain a better understanding of the symptoms, causes, treatments and other supports for specific mental illnesses that are common among adolescents

Major concepts addressed

- A mental illness changes a person's thinking, feelings or behaviour (or all three) and causes that person distress and difficulty in functioning
- Mental illness describes a broad range of conditions. The type, intensity, and duration of symptoms vary from person-to-person
- The exact cause of mental disorders is not known, but most experts believe that a combination of biological, psychological and environmental factors are involved
- Like illnesses that affect other parts of the body, mental illnesses are treatable, and the sooner people get proper treatment and supports, the better the outcomes
- With a variety of supports, most people with mental illness recover and go on to lead fulfilling and productive lives

Teacher background and preparation

- Read through the information sheets for Activity 2 on mental illnesses prior to the class
- Preview the PowerPoint presentation

MODULE 3

Activities

Activity 1:   PowerPoint presentation Part 2: (25 mins.)
What Happens When the Brain Gets Sick? The
Road to Recovery

Activity 2:   Specialist groups – Learning about specific mental
illnesses (15 mins.)

Activity 3:   Sharing the pieces (10 mins)

In advance

- Preview the PowerPoint presentation:
  Part 2: What Happens When the Brain Gets Sick? The Road to
  Recovery

- Photocopy Activity 2 handouts and informaion sheets on specific
  mental illnesses (there are 6 illnesses covered) one per student in
  six different groups e.g. if the class has 24 students, then
  photocopy 4 of each sheet

Materials required

- PowerPoint presentation Part 2: What happens when the brain gets
  sick: The road to recovery

- Handouts: Activity 2 Activity sheets

MODULE 3

Activity 1:   **(25 mins.)**

PowerPoint Presentation Part 2:
What Happens When the Brain Gets Sick? The Road to Recovery

Purpose:

- To provide an overview of the major mental illnesses that affect adolescents
  Group 1 Understanding Anxiety Disorders
  Group 2 Understanding ADHD
  Group 3 Understanding Bipolar Mood Disorder
  Group 4 Understanding Depression
  Group 5 Understanding Eating Disorders
  Group 6 Understanding Schizophrenia

- To continue exploring the idea of stigma and examine the impact it can have on the lives of people with mental illness.

- To show that there are effective treatments for mental illness, and that with appropriate supports, most people recover and lead fulfilling lives

How to:

- Use the web version of the presentation by logging on to:

  http://teenmentalhealth.org/curriculum/support-materials/

  The username is: **resource_user**
  The password is: **t33nh3alth**

  and Module 3/Activity 1: What Happens When the Brain Gets Sick? The Road to Recovery

- Play the presentation, pausing if needed.

MODULE 3

Specialist groups*

Purpose:

- To focus on some of the specific symptoms, treatments and supports for the major mental illnesses which affect adolescents
- To have students share information about the different disorders with other members of their class

How-to:

1) Explain to students that a jigsaw puzzle activity will be used during this lesson. This means that students will work in small groups and will become "experts" about one mental illness (one piece of the jigsaw). After completing the handout on their specific illness together, they will break up into mixed groups to share \ their information and learn more about the other illnesses from the other members of the group.

2) Give the 6 groups a few minutes to scan the information sheets. When they have finished reviewing, ask each group to discuss the nature of the mental illness they were assigned.

3) Have each group complete the handouts to share with others during the next activity. Remind them that they will each need to complete the activity sheets, as they will switch groups in the next activity.

* adapted from *MindMatters: Understanding Mental Illness*, pg 45

GROUP 1: Anxiety Disorders

What is anxiety?

Anxiety is a term which describes a normal feeling people experience when faced with threat or danger, or when stressed.

When people become anxious, they typically feel upset, uncomfortable and tense and may experience many physical symptoms such as stomach upset, shaking and headaches.

Feelings of anxiety are caused by experiences of life, such as a new relationship, a new job or school, illness or an accident.Feeling anxious is appropriate in these situations and usually we feel anxious for only a limited time. These feelings are not regarded as clinical anxiety, but are a part of everyday life.

What are anxiety disorders?

The anxiety disorders are a group of illnesses, each characterized by persistent feelings of intense anxiety. There are feelings of continual or extreme discomfort and tension, and may include panic attacks.

People are likely to be diagnosed with an anxiety disorder when their level of anxiety and feelings of panic are so extreme that they significantly interfere with daily life and stop them from doing what they want to do. This is what characterizes an anxiety disorder as more than normal feelings of anxiety.

Anxiety disorders affect the way the person thinks, feels and behaves and, if not treated, cause considerable suffering and distress. They often begin in adolescence or early adulthood and may sometimes be triggered by significant stress.

Anxiety disorders are common and may affect one in twenty people at any given time.

Anxiety Disorders - What are the main types of Anxiety Disorders?

All Anxiety Disorders are characterized by heightened anxiety or panic as well as significant problems in everyday life.

Generalized Anxiety Disorder

People with this disorder worry constantly about themselves or their loved ones, financial disaster, their health, work or personal relationships. These people experience continual apprehension and often suffer from many physical symptoms such as headache, diarrhea, stomach pains and heart palpitations.

Agoraphobia

Agoraphobia is fear of being in places or situations from which it may be difficult or embarrassing to get away, or a fear that help might be unavailable in the event of having a panic attack or panic symptoms.

People with agoraphobia most commonly experience fear in a cluster of situations: in supermarkets and department stores, crowded places of all kinds, confined spaces, public transport, elevators, highways and heights.

People experiencing agoraphobia may find comfort in the company of a safe person or object. This may be a spouse, friend, pet or medicine carried with them.

The onset of agoraphobia is common between the ages of 15 and 20, and is often associated with panic disorder or social phobia.

Panic Disorder (with or without agoraphobia)

People with this disorder experience panic attacks in situations where most people would not be afraid such as: at home, walking in the park or going to a movie. These attacks occur spontaneously, come on rapidly (over a few minutes) and go away slowly. Usually they last about 10-15 minutes.

The attacks are accompanied by all of the unpleasant physical symptoms of anxiety, with a fear that the attack may lead to death or a total loss of control.

It is because of this that some people start to experience a fear of going to places where panic attacks may occur and of being in places where help is not at hand. In addition to panic attacks and agoraphobia symptoms, people with panic disorder also worry about having another panic attack.

Specific Phobias

Everyone has some mild irrational fears, but phobias are intense fears about particular objects or situations which interfere with our lives. These might include fear of heights, water, dogs, closed spaces snakes or spiders.

Someone with a specific phobia is fine when the feared object is not present. However, when faced with the feared object or situation, the person can become highly anxious and experience a panic attack.

People affected by phobias can go to great lengths to avoid situations which would force them to confront the object or situation which they fear.

Social Phobia (also called social anxiety disorder)

People with Social Phobia fear that others will judge everything they do in a negative way and they feel easily embarrased in most social situations. They believe they may be considered to be flawed or worthless if any sign of poor performance is detected.

They cope by either trying to do everything perfectly, limiting what they are doing in front of others, especially eating, drinking, speaking or writing, or withdrawing gradually from contact with others. They will often experience panic symptoms in social situations and will avoid many situations where they feel observed by others (such as: in stores, movie theatres, public speaking and social events).

Obsessive Compulsive Disorder (OCD)

This disorder involves intrusive unwanted thoughts (obsessions) and the performance of elaborate rituals (compulsions) in an attempt to control or banish the persistent thoughts or to avoid feelings of unease.

The rituals are usually time consuming and seriously interfere with everyday life. For example, people may be constantly driven to wash their hands or continually return home to check that the door is locked or that the oven is turned off.

Anxiety Disorders

Post-Traumatic Stress Disorder (PTSD)

Some people who have experienced major traumas such as war, torture, hurricanes, earthquakes, accidents or personal violence may continue to feel terror long after the event is over.

They may experience nightmares or flashbacks for years. The flashbacks are often brought about by triggers related to the experience.

What causes Anxiety Disorders?

The causes of each disorder may vary, and it is not always easy to determine the causes in every case. All Anxiety Disorders are associated with abnormalities in the brain signaling mechanisms that are involved in the creation and expression of "normal" anxiety.

Personality

People with certain personality charactieristics may be more prone to Anxiety Disorders. Those who are easily upset, and are very sensitive, emotional or avoidant of others may be more likely to develop anxiety disorders, such as social phobia.

Learnt response

Some people exposed to situations, people or objects that are upsetting or Anxiety-producing may develop an anxiety response when faced with the same situation, person or object again, or become anxious when thinking about the situation, person or object.

Heredity

The tendancy to develop Anxiety Disorders runs in families and seems to have a genetic basis.

Biochemical processes

All Anxiety Disorders arise from disturbances in the different brain areas or processess that control Anxiety.

How can Anxiety Disorders be addressed?

Anxiety Disorders, if they are not effectively treated, may interfere significantly with a person's thinking and behaviour, causing considerable suffering and distress. Some Anxiety Disorders may precede depression or substance abuse and in such cases, treatment may help to prevent these problems.

Many professionals such as family doctors, psychologists, social workers, counsellors or psychiatrists can help people deal with anxiety disorders.

Treatment will often include education and specific types of psychotherapy (such as cognitive behavioural therapy) to help the person understand their thoughts, emotions and behaviour. People develop new ways of thinking about their Anxiety and how to deal more effectively with feelings of Anxiety.

Medication is sometimes used to help the person control their high anxiety levels, panic attacks or depression.

The benzodiazepines (like diazepam or valium) are used for the temporary relief of anxiety, but care has to be taken as these medications may occasionally cause dependence in some people.

Antidepressants play an important role in the treatment of some anxiety disorders, as well as associated or underlying depression. Contrary to common belief, antidepressants are not addictive.

MODULE 3

Group 1: Understanding Anxiety Disorders

What are Anxiety Disorders?

Who gets Anxiety Disorders and how common are they?

Describe some of the symptoms of Anxiety Disorders:

List and briefly explain some of the main types of Anxiety Disorders:

What type of treatment is available for people experiencing Anxiety Disorders?

What other kinds of support can help people with Anxiety Disorders recover?

GROUP 2: Attention Deficit Hyperactivity Disorder (ADHD)

What is Attention Deficit Hyperactivity Disorder (ADHD)?

Attention Deficit Hyperactivity Disorder is the most commonly diagnosed behavioural disorder of childhood.

In any six-month period, ADHD affects an estimated 4 -6 % of young people between the ages of 9 and 17. Boys are two to three times more likely then girls to develop ADHD. Although ADHD is usually associated with children, the disorder can persist into adulthood. Children and adults with ADHD are easily distracted by sights and sounds and other features of their environment, cannot concentrate for long periods of time, are restless and impulsive, or have a tendency to daydream and be slow to complete tasks.

Symptoms

The three predominant symptoms of ADHD are 1) inability to regulate activity level (hyperactivity); 2) inability to attend to tasks (inattention); and 3) impulsivity, or inability to inhibit behaviour.

Common symptoms include varying degrees of the following. All must occur with greater frequency and intensity than "normal" and must lead to functional impairment as a result of the symptoms in order to be considered ADHD:

- Poor concentration and brief attention span
- Increased activity - always on the go
- Impulsive - doesn't stop to think
- Social and relationship problems
- Fearless and takes undue risks
- Poor coordination
- Sleep problems
- Normal or high intelligence but under-performing at school

What causes ADHD?

While no one really knows what causes ADHD, it is generally agreed by the medical and scientific community that ADHD is due to problems in the brain's control of systems that regulate concentration, motivation and attention.

Much of today's research suggests that genetics plays a major role in ADHD. The possibility of a genetic cause to ADHD is supported by the fact that ADHD runs in families. Between 10 and 35 percent of children with ADHD have a first-degree relative with past or present ADHD. Approximately half of parents who have been diagnosed with ADHD themselves, will have a child with the disorder.

It has been generally considered that approximately 50% of ADHD cases can be explained by genetics. It is obvious that not every case of ADHD can be explained by genetics; it would seem that there are other causes.

Researchers have suggested that some of the following could also be responsible for ADHD symptoms:

- exposure to toxins (such as lead)
- injuries to the brain
- delayed brain maturation

However, all of these possibilities need further research.

Attention Deficit Hyperactivity Disorder (ADHD)

Myths, misunderstandings and facts

According to the National Institutes of Mental Health, ADHD is not caused by:

- Too much TV
- Sugar
- Caffeine
- Food colourings
- Poor home life
- Poor schools
- Damage to the brain from complications during birth
- Food allergies

How can ADHD be addressed?

A variety of medications and behavioural interventions are used to treat ADHD. The most effective treatments are medications. The most widely used medications are stimulants such as Ritalin. Nine out of ten children improve when taking one of these medications. When used as prescribed by qualified physicians, these medications are considered quite safe. Some common side effects are decreased appetite and insomnia. These side effects generally occur early in treatment and often decrease over time. Some studies have shown that the stimulants used to treat ADHD slow growth rate, but ultimate height is not affected.

Interventions used to help treat ADHD include several forms of psychotherapy, such as cognitive-behavioural therapy, social skills training, support groups, and parent and educator skills training. A combination of medication and psychotherapy may be more effective than medication treatment alone in improving social skills, parent-child relations, reading achievement and aggressive symptoms.

MODULE 3

Group 2: Understanding Attention Deficit Hyperactivity Disorder (ADHD)

What is ADHD?

Who gets ADHD and how common is it?

Describe some of the symptoms of ADHD:

What type of treatment is available for people experiencing ADHD?

What other kinds of support can help people with ADHD recover?

GROUP 3: Bipolar Mood Disorder

Bipolar Mood Disorder is the new name for what was called manic depressive illness. The new name is used as it better describes the extreme mood swings - from depression and sadness to elation and excitement – that people with this illness experience.

People with Bipolar Mood Disorder experience recurrent episodes of depressed and elated moods. Both can be mild to severe.

The term 'mania' is used to describe elation and overactivity.

Some people with bipolar disorder only have episodes of elation and excitement.

What are the symptoms of Bipolar Mood Disorder?

Mania - Common symptoms include varying degrees of the following:

- **Elevated mood** – The person feels extremely high, happy and full of energy. The experience is often described as feeling on top of the world and being invincible.

- **Increased energy and overactivity**

- **Reduced need for sleep**

- **Irritability** – The person may easily and frequently get angry and irritable with people who disagree or dismiss their sometimes unrealistic plans of ideas.

- **Rapid thinking and speech** – Thoughts are more rapid than usual. This can lead to the person speaking quickly and jumping from subject-to-subject.

- **Lack of inhibitions** – This can be the result of the person's reduced ability to foresee the consequences of their actions, for example, spending large amounts of money buying things they don't really need.

- **Grandiose plans and beliefs** – It is common for people experiencing mania to believe that they are unusually talented or gifted or are kings, movie stars or political leaders. It is common for religious beliefs to intensify or for people with this illness to believe they are an important religious figure.

- **Lack of insight** – A person experiencing mania may understand that other people see their ideas and actions as inappropriate, reckless or irrational. However, they are unlikely to recognize the behaviour as inappropriate in themselves.

- **Psychosis** – Some people with mania or depression experience psychotic symptoms such as hallucinations and delusions.

Depression

- Many people with Bipolar Mood Disorder experience depressive episodes. This type of Depression can be triggered by a stressful event, but more commonly occurs without obvious cause.

- The person loses interest and pleasure in activities they previously enjoyed. They may withdraw and stop seeing friends, avoid social activities and cease simple tasks such as shopping and showering.

- They may become overwhelmed by a deep Depression, lose their appetite, lose weight, become unable to concentrate, and may experience feelings of guilt or hopelessness.

- Some attempt suicide because they believe life has become meaningless or they feel too guilty to go on.

- Others develop false beliefs (delusions) of persecution or guilt, or think that they are evil.

- For more information on depression and its treatment, please see the information sheets called "What is depression?"

- Some attempt suicide because they believe life has become meaningless or they feel too guilty to go on.

- Others develop false beliefs (delusions) of persecution or guilt, or think that they are evil.

Bipolar Mood Disorder (cont.)

Depression (cont.)

- For more information on depression and its treatment, please see the information sheets called "What is Depression?"

Normal moods

Most people who have episodes of mania and depression experience normal moods in between. They are able to live productive lives, manage household and business commitments and hold down a job.

Everyone experiences mood swings from time-to-time. It is when these moods become extreme and lead to a failure to cope with life that medical attention is necessary.

What causes Bipolar Mood Disorder?

Bipolar Mood Disorder affects one to two people in every hundred in the Canadian population. Men and women have an equal chance of developing the disorder. It usually appears when people are in their twenties, but often begins in the teen years.

It is believed that Bipolar Mood Disorder is caused by a combination of factors including genetics, biochemistry, stress and its onset may even be related to the seasons.

Genetic factors

Studies on close relations, identical twins and adopted children whose natural parents have Bipolar Mood Disorder strongly suggest that the illness may be genetically transmitted, and that children of parents with Bipolar Mood Disorder have a greater risk of developing the disorder.

Biochemical factors

Mania, like major depression, is believed to be associated with chemical changes or other problems in the brain which can often be corrected with medication.

Stress

Stress may play an important role in triggering symptoms, but not always. Sometimes the illness itself may cause the stressful event (such as divorce or a failed business), which may then be blamed for causing the illness. Drugs or other physical stressors (such as jet lag) may bring on an episode.

Seasons

Mania is more common in the spring, and Depression in the early winter. The reason for this is not clear, but it is thought to be associated with the light/dark cycle.

How can bipolar disorder be addressed?

- Effective treatments are available for depressive and manic episodes of Bipolar Mood Disorder. Medications called thymoleptics (such as lithium) are an essential treatment for the entire course of the illness.

- For the depressive phase of the illness, antidepressant medications are effective. Bright light therapy and some psychological treatments may also help.

- Antidepressants are not addictive. They slowly return the balance of neurotransmitters in the brain, taking one to four weeks to achieve their positive effects.

- Medication should be adjusted only under medical supervision, as some people may experience a switch to a manic phase if given an antidepressant.

- During acute or severe attacks of mania, several different medications may be used. Some are specifically used to calm the person's manic excitement: others are used to help stabilize the person's mood. Medications such as lithium are also used as preventive measures, as they help to control mood swings and reduce the frequency and severity of both depressive and manic phases.

- It may be necessary to admit a person with severe depression or mania to a hospital for a time.

- When people are in a manic phase, it can often be difficult to persuade them that they need treatment.

- Psychotherapy and counseling are used with medication to help the person understand the illness and better manage its effects on their life.

- With access to appropriate treatment and support, most people with bipolar mood disorder lead full and productive lives.

Group 3: Understanding Bipolar Mood Disorder

What is Bipolar Mood Disorder?

Who gets Bipolar Mood Disorder and how common is it?

Describe some of the symptoms of Bipolar Mood Disorder:

What combination of factors is believed to cause Bipolar Mood Disorder?

What type of treatment is available for people experiencing Bipolar Mood Disorder?

What other kinds of support can help a person with Bipolar Mood Disorder recover?

GROUP 4: Depression

What is Depression?

The word Depression is often used to describe the feelings of sadness which all of us experience at some times in our lives. It is also a term used to describe a form of mental illness called clinical Depression. Clinical Depression is not sadness.

Because Depression is so common, it is important to understand the difference between unhappiness or sadness in daily life and the symptoms of clinical Depression.

When faced with stress, such as the loss of a loved one, relationship breakdown or great disappointment or frustration, most people will feel unhappy or sad. These are emotional reactions which are appropriate to the situation and will usually last only a limited time. These reactions are not a Clinical Depression, but are part of everyday life.

The term Clinical Depression describes not just one illness, but a group of illnesses characterized by excessive or long-term depressed mood which affects the person's life. Clinical Depression is often accompanied by feelings of anxiety. Whatever the symptoms and causes of Clinical Depression, there are many therapeutic interventions which are effective.

What are the main types of depressive illness?

Adjustment disorders with depressed mood

People with this problem are reacting to distressing situations in their lives (e.g., the failure of a close relationship or loss of a job) but to a greater degree than usual.

This Depression is more intense than the unhappiness experienced in daily life. It lasts longer and the symptoms often include anxiety, poor sleep and a loss of appetite. This form of depression may last longer than a few weeks.

It usually goes away when the cause is removed or the person finds a new way to cope with the stress. Occasionally people require professional help to overcome this type of Depression.

"Baby Blues" and postpartum depression

The so-called "baby blues" affect about half of all new mothers. They feel mildly depressed, anxious, tense or unwell, and may have difficulty sleeping even though they are tired and lethargic most of the time. These feelings may last only hours or a few days, then disappear. Professional help is not usually needed.

However, in up to ten percent of mothers this feeling of sadness develops into a serious disorder called postpartum depression. Mothers with this illness find it increasingly difficult to cope with the demands of everyday life.

They can experience anxiety, fear, despondency and sadness. Some mothers may have panic attacks or become tense and irritable. There may be a change in appetite and sleep patterns. Because of these symptoms they may have difficulties in their daily lives, including trouble in caring for their child.

A severe, but rare form of postpartum Depression is called puerperal psychosis. The woman is unable to cope with her everyday life and is disturbed in her thinking and behaviour. Professional help is needed for both postpartum depression and puerperal psychosis.

Major Depressive Disorder

This is the most common form of clinical depression. It can come on without apparent cause, although in some cases a severely distressing event might trigger the condition.

The cause is not well understood but is believed to be associated with a chemical imbalance or other problem in the parts of the brain that control mood. Genetic predisposition is common.

A depressive episode can develop in people who have coped well with life, who are good at their work, and happy in family and social relationships.

For no apparent reason, they can become low-spirited, lose their enjoyment of life and suffer disturbed sleep patterns. People experiencing a Depressive episode

Depression (cont.)

Major Depressive Disorder (cont.)

Sometimes the feelings of hopelessness and despair can lead to thoughts of suicide. Suicide is an tragic outcome of depression in some people.

The most serious form of this type of Depression is called psychotic depression. During this illness, the person loses touch with reality, may stop eating and drinking and may hear voices saying they are wicked or worthless or deserve to be punished.

Others develop false beliefs (delusions) that they have committed bad deeds in the past and deserve to be punished, or falsely believe that they have a terminal illness such as cancer, despite there being no medical evidence.

A depressive episode or psychotic Depression are serious illnesses which present risks to the person's life and well-being. Professional assessment and treatment is always necessary and, in severe cases, hospitalization may be required for a period of time.

Bipolar Mood Disorder (previously called Manic Depression)

A person with bipolar mood disorder experiences depressive episodes (as described above) with periods of mania which involve extreme happiness, overactivity, rapid speech, a lack of inhibition and in more serious instances, psychotic symptoms including hearing voices and delusions of gandeur.

Sometimes only periods of mania occur, without depressive episodes, but this is rare. More information about this mood disorder is found in the section called "What is bipolar mood disorder?"

What causes Depression?

Often there are many interrelated factors associated with Depression.

Heredity: It is well established that the tendency to develop depression runs in families. This is similar to a predisposition to other illnesses, such as heart disease and high blood pressure.

Biochemical imbalance: Depressive episodes are thought to be due in part to a chemical imbalance or other problems in the brain. This can be corrected with anti-depressant medication or with psychotherapy.

Stress: Depression may also be associated with stress after personal tragedies or disasters. It is more common at certain stages of life, such as at childbirth. It may also occur with some physical illnesses.

Personality: People with certain personality characteristics may be more prone to depression.

Some people have a low grade depressive disorder called dysthymia which may become difficult to distinguish from their personality.

How can Depression be addressed?

People experiencing symptoms of depression which have persisted for a long time, or which are affecting their life to a great extent, should contact their family doctor or community health centre. Modern methods for dealing with depression can help the person return to more normal feelings and to enjoy life. The approach depends on each person's symptoms and circumstances, but will generally take one or more of the following forms:

- Psychological interventions help individuals understand their thoughts, behaviours and interpersonal relationships.

- Antidepressant medications relieve depressed feelings, restore normal sleep patterns and appetite, and reduce anxiety. Antidepressant medications are not addictive. They slowly return the balance of neurotransmitters in the brain, taking one to four weeks to achieve their positive effects.

- Specific medications help to manage mood swings for people with bipolar illness.

- General supportive counseling assists people in sorting out practical problems and conflicts, and helps them understand how to cope with their depression.

- Lifestyle changes such as physical exercise may help people who suffer from Depression.

- For some severe forms of Depression, electroconvulsive therapy (ECT) is a safe and effective treatment. While it is still considered by some to be controversial, it may be lifesaving for people who are psychotic, at high risk of suicide, or who, because of the severity of their illness, have stopped eating or drinking and may die as a result.

MODULE 3

Group 4: Understanding Depression

What is Depression?

Who gets Depression and how common is it?

Describe some of the symptoms of Depression:

List and briefly describe some of the main types of Depression:

What type of treatment is available for people experiencing Depression?

What other kinds of support can help a person with Depression recover?

GROUP 5: Eating Disorders

What are Eating Disorders?

Anorexia Nervosa (AN) and Bulimia Nervosa (BN) are the two most common serious eating disorders. Each illness involves a preoccupation with control over body weight, eating and food. Sometimes they occur together.

- People with Anorexia are determined to control the amounts of food they eat

- People with Bulimia tend to feel out of control about food

Anorexia Nervosa may affect up to one in every two hundred teenage girls, although the illness can be experienced earlier and later in life. Most people who
have Anorexia Nervosa are female, but males can also develop the disorder.

Bulimia Nervosa may affect up to two in every hundred teenage girls. More females than males develop Bulimia.

While these rates show that few people meet the criteria for eating disorders, it is far more common for people to have unrealistic attitudes about body size and shape. These attitudes may contribute to inappropriate eating or dieting practices, such as fad dieting, which is not the same as having an eating disorder.

Both illnesses can be overcome and it is important for the person to seek advice about treatment for either condition as early as possible.

What are the symptoms of Anorexia Nervosa? (AN)

Anorexia nervosa is characterized by:

- A loss of at least 15% of body weight resulting from refusal to eat enough food

- Refusal to maintain minimally normal body weight

- An intense fear of becoming 'fat' even though the person is underweight

- Cessation of menstrual periods

- Misperception of body image, so that people see themselves as fat when they're really very thin

- A preoccupation with the preparation of food

- Unusual rituals and activities pertaining to food, such as making lists of 'good' and 'bad' food and hiding food.

Usually Anorexia Nervosa begins with a weight loss, resulting from dieting. It is not known why some people go on to develop AN while others do not. As weight decreases, the person's ability to appropriately judge their body size and make proper decisions about their eating also decreases.

About 40% of people with Anorexia Nervosa will later develop Bulimia Nervosa.

What are the symptoms of Bulimia Nervosa? (BN)

Bulimia Nervosa is characterized by:

- Eating binges, which involve consumption of large amounts of calorie-rich food, during which the person feels a loss of personal control and following which the person feels self disgust

- Attempts to compensate for binges and to avoid weight gain by self-induced vomiting, and/or abuse of laxatives and diuretics

- Strong concerns about body shape and weight

A person with BN is usually average or slightly above average weight for height, so it is often less recognizable than the person with AN.

BN often starts with rigid weight reduction dieting in

Eating Disorders

an attempt to reach 'thinness'. Inadequate nutrition causes tiredness and the person develops powerful urges to binge eat.

Vomiting after a binge seems to bring a sense of relief, but this is temporary and soon turns to distress and guilt. Some people use laxatives, apparently unaware that laxatives do not reduce calorie or fat content, and serve only to eliminate nutritionally vital trace elements and to dehydrate the body.

The person can make frantic efforts to break from the pattern, but the vicious binge/purge/exercise cycle, and the feelings associated with it, may have become compulsive and uncontrollable.

A person with bulimia may experience chemical imbalances in the body which bring about lethargy, depression and clouded thinking.

What causes Anorexia Nervosa and Bulimia Nervosa?

The causes of AN and BN remain unclear. Biological, psychological and social factors may be involved. While there are many hypotheses about various social and psychological factors involved in AN, there is no good scientific evidence which shows causality for one particular pathway.

What are the effects of Anorexia Nervosa and Bulimia Nervosa?

Physical effects

The physical effects can be serious, but are often reversible if the illnesses are tackled early. If left untreated, severe AN and BN can be life-threatening. Responding to early warning signs and obtaining early treatment is essential.

Both illnesses, when severe, can cause:

- Harm to kidneys
- Urinary tract infections and damage to the colon
- Dehydration, constipation and diarrhea
- Seizures, muscle spasms or cramps
- Chronic indigestion
- Loss of menstruation or irregular periods
- Heart palpitations

Many of the effects of anorexia are related to malnutrition, including:

- Absence of menstrual periods
- Severe sensitivity to cold
- Growth of down-like hair all over the body
- Inability to think rationally and to concentrate

Severe bulimia is likely to cause:

- Erosion of dental enamel from vomiting
- Swollen salivary glands
- The possibility of a ruptured stomach
- Chronic sore throat

Eating Disorders (cont.)

Emotional and psychological effects:

These are likely to include

- Difficulty with activities which involve food
- Loneliness, due to self-imposed isolation and a reluctance to develop personal relationships
- Deceptive behaviours related to food
- Fear of the disapproval of others if the illness becomes known, mixed with the hope that family and friends might intervene and offer help
- Mood swings, changes in personality, emotional outbursts or depression

How can eating disorders be addressed?

Changes in eating behaviour may be caused by several illnesses other than AN or BN, so a thorough medical examination by a medical practitioner is the first step.

Once the illness has been diagnosed, a range of health practitioners can be involved in treatment, because the illness affects people both physically and mentally. Professionals involved in treatment may include psychiatrists, psychologists, physicians, dietitians, social workers, occupational therapists and nurses.

Outpatient treatment and attendance in special programs are the preferred method of treatment for people with AN. Hospitalization may be necessary for those who are severely malnourished.

Treatment can include medication to assist severe depression and to correct hormonal and chemical imbalances. BN may respond to specific antidepressant medications.

Dietary education assists with retraining in healthy eating habits.

Counselling and specific therapies such as (cognitivebehavioural therapy) are used to help change unhealthy thoughts about eating, The ongoing support of family and friends is essential.

MODULE 3

Group 5: Understanding Eating Disorders

What are eating disorders?

Who gets eating disorders and how common are they?

Describe some of the symptoms of Anorexia Nervosa (AN) and Bulimia Nervosa (BN):

What are the physical, emotional and psychological effects of AN and BN?

What type of treatment is available for people experiencing AN and BN?

What other kinds of support can help people with eating disorders recover?

GROUP 6: Schizophrenia

What is Schizophrenia?

Schizophrenia is a mental illness which affects one person in every hundred. Schizophrenia interferes with a person's mental functioning and behaviour, and in the long term may cause changes to their personality.

The first onset of schizophrenia is usually in adolescence or early adulthood. Some people may experience only one or more brief episodes of psychosis in their lives, and it may not develop into schizophrenia. For others, it may remain a recurrent or life-long condition.

The onset of the illness may be rapid, with acute symptoms developing over several weeks, or more commonly, it may be slow, developing over months or even years.

During onset, the person often withdraws from others, gets depressed and anxious, and develops unusual fears or obsessions.

Schizophrenia is characterized by two different sets of symptoms. Positive symptoms refers to symptoms that appear - like delusions (thinking things that aren't true), or hallucinations (seeing or hearing things that aren't there).

Negative symptoms refer to things that are taken away by the illness, so that a person has less energy, less pleasure and interest in normal life activities, spending less time with friends, being less able to think clearly.

What are the symptoms of schizophrenia?
Positive symptoms of schizophrenia include:

Delusions – false beliefs of persecution, guilt or grandeur, or being under outside control. These beliefs will not change regardless of the evidence against them. People with schizophrenia may describe outside plots against them or think they have special powers or gifts. Sometimes they withdraw from people or hide to avoid imagined persecution.

Hallucinations – most commonly involving hearing voices. Other less common experiences can include seeing, feeling, tasting or smelling things, which to the person are real but which are not actually there.

Thought disorder – where the speech may be difficult to follow, for example, jumping from one subject to another with no logical connection. Thoughts and speech may be jumbled and disjointed. The person may think someone is interfering with their mind.

Other symptoms of Schizophrenia include:

Loss of drive – when the ability to engage in everyday activities such as washing and cooking is lost. This lack of drive, initiative or motivation is part of the illness and is not laziness.

Blunted expression of emotions – where the ability to express emotion is greatly reduced and is often accompanied by a lack of response or an inappropriate response to external events such as happy or sad occasions.

Social withdrawal – this may be caused by a number of factors including the fear that someone is going to harm them, or a fear of interacting with others because of a loss of social skills.

Lack of insight or awareness of other conditions – because some experiences such as delusions or hallucinations are so real, it is common for people with schizophrenia to be unaware they are ill. For this and other reasons, such as medication side-effects, they may refuse to accept treatment which could be essential for their well being.

Thinking difficulties – a person's concentration, memory and ability to plan and organize may be affected, making it more difficult to reason, communicate, and complete daily tasks.

What causes Schizophrenia?

No single cause has been identified, but several factors are believed to contribute to the onset of schizophrenia.

Psychotic Disorders / Schizophrenia (cont.)

Genetic factors – A predisposition to Schizophrenia can run in families. In the general population, only one percent of people develop it over their lifetime. If one parent suffers from schizophrenia, the children have a ten percent chance of developing the condition – and a ninety percent chance of not developing it.

Biochemical factors – Certain biochemical substances in the brain are involved in this condition, especially a neurotransmitter called dopamine. One likely cause of this chemical disturbance is the person's genetic predisposition to

Family relationships – No evidence has been found to support the suggestion that family relationships cause the illness. However, some people with Schizophrenia are sensitive to family tensions which, for them, may be associated with relapses.

Environment – It is well-recognized that stressful incidents often precede the diagnosis of schizophrenia; they can act as precipitating events in vulnerable people. People with schizophrenia often become anxious, irritable and unable to concentrate before any acute symptoms are evident. This can cause relationships to deteriorate, possibly leading to divorce or unemployment. Often these factors are blamed for the onset of the illness when, in fact, the illness itself has caused the crisis. There is some evidence that environmental factors that damage brain development (such as a viral illness in utero) may lead to schizophrenia later in life.

Drug use – The use of some drugs, such as cannabis (marijuana), LSD, Crack and crystal meth is likely to cause a relapse in schizophrenia. Occasionally, severe drug use may lead to or "unmask" schizophrenia.

Myths, misunderstandings and facts

Myths, misunderstandings, negative stereotypes and attitudes surround the issue of mental illness in general, and in particular, schizophrenia. They result in stigma, discrimination and isolation.

Do people with Schizophrenia have a split personality?
No. Schizophrenia refers to the change in the person's mental function, where the thoughts and perceptions become disordered.

Are people with Schizophrenia intellectually disabled? No. The illness is not an intellectual disability.

Are people with Schizophrenia dangerous?
No, people with Schizophrenia are generally not dangerous when receiving appropriate treatment. However, a minority of people with the illness may become aggressive when experiencing an untreated acute episode, or if they are taking illicit drugs. This is usually expressed to family and friends, rarely to strangers.

Is Schizophrenia a life-long mental disorder?
Like many mental illnesses, Schizophrenia is usually lifelong. However, most people, with professional help and social support, learn to manage their symptoms and have a satisfactory quality of life. About 20-30 percent of people with schizophrenia have only one or two psychotic episodes in their lives.

How can Schizophrenia and psychosis be addressed?

The most effective treatment for schizophrenia involves medication, psychological counseling and help with managing its impact on everyday life.

The sooner that Schizophrenia is treated, the better the long-term prognosis or outcome. The opposite is also true: the longer schizophrenia is left untreated, and the more psychotic breaks are experienced by someone with the illness, the lower the level of eventual recovery. Early intervention is key to helping people recover.

Psychotic Disorders / Schizophrenia (cont.)

How can schizophrenia and psychosis be addressed? (cont)

The development of antipsychotic medications has revolutionized the treatment of schizophrenia. Now, most people can be treated and remain in the community instead of in hospital.

Antipsychotic medications work by correcting the brain chemistry associated with the illness. New but well-tested medications are emerging which may promote a more complete recovery with fewer side effects than the older versions.

Schizophrenia is an illness, like many physical illnesses. Just as insulin is a lifeline for people with diabetes, antipsychotic medications can be a lifeline for a person with schizophrenia. Just as with diabetes, some people will need to take medication indefinitely to prevent a relapse and keep symptoms under control.

Though there is no known cure for schizophrenia, regular contact with a doctor or psychiatrist and other mental health professionals such as nurses, occupational therapists and psychologists can help a person with schizophrenia recover and get on with their lives. Informal supports such as self-help and social support are also very important to recovery. Meaningful activity or employment, and adequate housing and income are all essential to keeping people healthy.

Sometimes specific therapies directed toward symptoms such as delusions may also be useful.

Counselling and social support can help people with schizophrenia overcome problems with finances, housing, work, socializing and interpersonal relationships.

With effective treatment and support, most people with schizophrenia can lead fulfilling and productive lives.

MODULE 3

Group 6: Understanding Schizophrenia

What is Schizophrenia?

Who gets Schizophrenia and how common is it?

Describe some of the symptoms of Schizophrenia:

List and briefly explain some of the factors that contribute to the onset of Schizophrenia:

What type of treatment is available for people with Schizophrenia?

What other kinds of support can help people with Schizophrenia recover?

MODULE 3

Activity 3: (10 mins.)

Sharing the pieces

Purpose:

In this activity, the "student experts" will share their new knowledge about their mental illness with others in the class. In this way, each student will gain an increased understanding of the mental illnesses covered in the unit.

How to:

1) Form new, mixed groups which include at least one member from each of the illness-specific groups.

2) Give each student two minutes to report to the newly-formed group about their specific area of mental illness, highlighting important points about how common the illness is, symptoms and effective supports and treatments.

It may be a good idea to invite the school counselor to sit in with your class when you show the video. If that's not possible, you should inform them about the nature and content of the video (or make a copy available to them) in case students approach them afterward.

Experiences of mental illness

Overview:

In this module students will hear directly from other young people about their personal experiences with mental illness. In their own words, a number of young people describe their symptoms, the difficulties they went through as a result of their illness, and how the illness affected their lives at school, within their families, and in their friendships.

Students will work together in small groups to explore the impact of mental illnesses on the lives of the young people in the video.

Learning objectives:

- To recognize, on a more personal level, the way mental illnesses can impact on a person's life
- To appreciate the importance of getting help and proper treatment

Major concepts addressed:

- Mental illnesses are diseases that affect many aspects of a person's life
- While they are usually lifelong, mental illnesses are often episodic and with effective treatment, most people can function well in everyday life

Teacher background and preparation

Teachers should preview Module 4 in the support materials. The review the video Courageous Not Crazy: Experiences of Mental Illness, before showing it to the class.Reviewing the video in advance will help you become familiar with the content so that you can then help students identify and keep track of the individual they are to focus on while watching the video.

The support materials are located on:
http://teenmentalhealth.org/curriculum/support-materials/

The username is: **resource_user**
The password is: **t33nh3alth**

V

Remind the students that the video they are about to watch was created by youth at Laing House, a peer support centre for young people with mental illness in Halifax, NS. The youth were in charge of every aspect of the video, from planning and production to editing and sound mixing.

In advance:

- Decide whether you will show the video to the class as a whole or you want smaller groups to view the video through the web-based format.

- Set up computer work stations
- Photocopy Activity 1 Video discussion sheet (1 copy of each per student).

Activities

Activity 1: Experiences of mental illness video and activity sheet (40 mins.)

Materials required:

- Web-based video of Courageous Not Crazy: Experiences of Mental Illness
- Handout: Activity 1 Video discussion sheet.

MODULE 4

V

Discussion of the video may raise the issue of youth suicide. While this discussion is appropriate within the broader context of mental illness, it is important that the discussion not become focused on suicide. Any discussion of suicide should:

• avoid portraying suicide as romantic, heroic or tragic;

• avoid increasing knowledge about methods of suicide;

• emphasize the importance of seeking help and of everyone's responsibility to tell a trusted adult if a friend mentions thoughts of suicide, even if that person asks for it to be kept a secret.

Activity 1: (40 mins.)

Experiences of mental illness video and discussion sheet

Purpose:

• To explore the impact of mental illnesses on a group of young people

• To look specifically at the experience of each character in the video through small group work

How to:

1) Inform the class that the video they are about to see was created by young people who have experienced mental illness, and is about their experiences.

Before showing the video, divide the class into 5 groups and distribute the video activity sheet. Allocate each group one of the characters in the video (Chris, Tim, Sheila, Tyrone or Aaron).

Give the students a few minutes to read through the questions on the video discussion sheet. Explain that each group will focus specifically on one character and their particular diagnosis and experience, but that they will watch the complete video and hear the stories of all of the individuals.

2) Play Courageous not Crazy: Experiences of Mental Illness. Remind each group about which individual they should be focusing on while watching.

3) After viewing the video, ask students to get together in their smaller groups and complete the group questions. Ask one member of the group to record the answers so that they can be shared with the whole class afterwards. Help students understand that the video may not include direct answers by each individual for each of the questions, but that they can make inferences from what the individuals said. Circulate among the teams to listen as they discuss their answers, and provide guidance if teams are confused about how to answer the questions.

4) Bring the groups back together and ask a member of each group to summarize the discussion from each of the small groups for the class.

cont. >

V

The most important concept for students to grasp through the class discussion is that although the individuals in the video had different mental illnesses and different experiences, there are some common themes and concerns for each character. Prompt students to think about the similarities among the individuals that are brought up.

How to (cont.)

5) Using the questions below, facilitate a discussion with the whole class:
   a) What specific illnesses were mentioned in the video?
   b) Describe how some of the characters appear to have lost touch with reality.
   c) What help or treatment did the characters receive?
   d) Did the characters recover? What do you mean by "recover"?
   e) Are there other mental illnesses you have heard about? What mental illnesses are you aware of that were not mentioned in the video?

6) Conclude the activity by addressing any questions that students may have after watching the video. Can students see any similarities among the individuals in the video, even though they have different mental illlnesses?

Video Discussion Sheet

Name of your character:

What mental illness does the person have?

When did it start?

How did the illness affect the person's thoughts, feelings and behaviours?

Did the illness cause the person difficulty in his or her life? In what ways?

What kind of treatment did the individual get?

How has the individual's life changed since getting treatment?

What kinds of things have helped the person recover and stay well?

What other questions would you like to ask your character in order to better understand their illness?

Seeking help and finding support

Overview

How do we decide that what a person is experiencing is outside the range of the normal ups and downs we all go through? When is it time to seek assistance from professionals?

Seeking help and finding support for mental health issues can be a tricky business. From the outside, it's often not clear when intervention is necessary, and people who are experiencing distress may themselves not always be aware of what's going on, and can be reluctant to come forward for fear of being labeled.

When people know that they will not be discriminated against or harassed, they are much more likely to seek help. Early intervention is important and increases the chances of a quick recovery.

This lesson will address the issues around help seeking, as well as providing ideas about ways in which that help and support can be accessed, within the school and beyond.

Learning Objectives

- To understand that people need support to deal with stressful life events and situations
- To learn to distinguish between "normal" responses to stress and difficulty, and those that may indicate a need for additional support from professionals
- To get students to consider who they could talk to if they were worried about their own mental health, or that of a friend or relative
- To identify support personnel in the school relevant to mental health
- To become familiar with the range of community-based healthcare services and groups available to support people who are experiencing mental illness and their families and friends

Major Concepts Addressed

- Mental illnesses, like chronic physical illnesses, can be effectively addressed
- Stigma acts as a barrier to people seeking help for mental health concerns
- Getting help early increases the chances that a person will make a full recovery from mental illness
- Recovery from mental illness is possible, when a range of supports, beyond formal treatment, are available

MODULE 5

Teacher Background and Preparation

- Read through all activities and handouts before class
- Preview video Courageous Not Crazy: Help and Support
- Compile list of community mental health resources for students

Activities

Activity 1: Video and activity sheet: Help and support – Youth Experiences (15 mins.)
Activity 2: Getting Help (15 mins.)
Activity 3: Support Strategies (10 mins.)

In Advance

- Fill out template of community mental health resources
- Preview video
- Set up computer(s) to view video
- Photocopy handouts for Activity 1 Video activity sheets, Activity 2 What if... scenarios, Checklists 1, 2 and 3, Activity 3 Support strategies (one for each student)
- Cut Activity 2: What if...scenarios into cards

Materials Required

- Web-based video of Courageous Not Crazy: Help and Support
- Handouts: Activity 1 Video activity sheets, Activity 2 What if... scenarios, Checklists 1, 2 and 3, Activity 3 Support strategies

Template - **Community Mental Health Resources**

The following mental health related resources are available in many communities including youth oriented programmes. Find out the contact information for these resources in your community and distribute to students. Your local CMHA branch can provide assistance.

School Resources:

- Guidance counselor
- Social worker
- Nurse
- Peer support

Local Community Resources:

- Crisis/distress lines
- Mental health lines
- Youth centres
- Drop-ins
- Community health centres
- Hospitals/clinics
- First episode centres
- Peer support groups

Mental Health Organizations (Provincial and National):

- Canadian Mental Health Association (www.cmha.ca)
- Centre for Addiction and Mental Health (www.camh.net)
- Mood Disorders Society of Canada (www.mooddisorderscanada.ca)
- Schizophrenia Society of Canada (www.schizophrenia.ca)
- Anxiety Disorders Association of Canada (www.anxietycanada.ca)
- Teen Mental Health (www.teenmentalhealth.org)

Kids Help Phone – 1-800-668-6868
www.kidshelppphone.ca

Kids Help Phone is Canada's only 24-hour, national bilingual telephone counseling service for children and youth. Provides counseling directly to children and youth directly between the ages of 4 and 19 years and helps adults aged 20 and over to find the counseling services they need.

Remind students that communicating their concerns about coping and dealing with mental health and other difficulties is really hard, and takes a lot of courage.

It's a good idea to anticipate potential student disclosures and to be prepared to deal properly with these situations. Ask the school social worker or a CMHA public educator to be on hand if possible.

Activity 1: (15 min.)

Video Activity Sheet: Courageous Not Crazy: Help and Support

Purpose:

- To learn more about young people's real life experiences getting help to deal with their mental health problems

How to:

1) Explain to the class that you will be watching a video made by youth from Laing House (in Halifax, Nova Scotia), which focuses on their experiences getting help and finding support to deal with their illness.

   Hand out the activity sheets and give the class a minute or two to read over the questions. Tell them that they are not expected to take notes while they're watching the video, but should keep the questions in mind as they watch, so that they can discuss the answers afterward.

2) Show the video and discuss the students' answers to the questions as a group.

   Conclude the activity by addressing any questions that students may have after watching the video. Ask students if they can see any similarties among the different individuals, even though they have different mental illnesses.

MODULE 5

Courageous Not Crazy Part 3: Help and Support

How did the youth in the video find help?

Did their friends and family notice there was something going on? What did they notice?

Did any of the youth talk to school staff like teachers or counsellors?

What does it mean to be supportive?

Did any of the youth attend a self-help or peer support group? If so, what was that like for them?

What kinds of supports/services seemed to help the most?

How can you help a friend?

Activity 2: (15 mins.)

Getting help*

Purpose:

- To describe a range of scenarios in which it would be important to tell or refer a problem to an appropriate adult.

How-to:

1) Explain to students that they will be engaging in a problem-solving lesson in which they can speculate about the possible actions they could take in a range of situations involving young people in distress. They will explore the scenarios using a game.

2) Ask students to arrange themselves into groups of four to six. Get them to sit in a circle – on the floor might be easiest.

3) Hand out the set of cards from the Activity Sheet: What if... scenarios. Ask each group to lay out their What if... cards in a circle with enough room inside the circle to spin a bottle or pen.

4) In turn, each of the participants takes a spin, and reads out the card the bottle points to. The person whose turn it is speculates first about what to do in such a situation, then others help out by adding their views, questions or challenges.

5) When they have finished discussing the scenarios, ask the class to come back together and pose the following questions:

   - Was there any disagreement in the groups about what was best to do?

   - Which was the scenario most likely to actually happen out of those you discussed?

   - Which do you think would be the hardest scenario to deal with if it happened to you or a friend or family member?

   - What sorts of fears or concerns would stop people from seeking help or telling someone else in these situations?

   - What kinds of things would motivate someone to seek help or tell someone their concerns in the situations you discussed?

6) Distribute "Something's not quite right" checklists and read them through with the class.

---

*Adapted from Lesson 4 of Coping - *MindMatters*.

MODULE 5

What if.........scenarios

1 Your friend seems really down and talks about dropping out of school.

2 A friend has been on a long diet, is getting really skinny and never seems to eat. She thinks she's really fat and will not wear shorts or a bathing suit.

3 Since your dad left, your brother/sister is spending almost all of their time smoking, drinking and watching TV, never wanting to do anything else. You have not told your friends about your parents splitting up.

4 There is a situation at school that is really stressing you out. Everyday when you wake up, you remember the situation and start to feel sick.

5 Your friend says s/he would be better off if s/he ran away. Your friend has already been sleeping over at your house a lot lately.

6 Someone in your class has started smoking marijuana before school everyday. The friends who smoke with this person only do it occasionally on the weekends. People are joking about how s/he is behaving – out of it and spacey. The person seems pretty down to you.

7 Your friend has started taking different kinds of pills at school, and is asking other people for painkillers all the time.

8 Your friend isn't acting like his old self. He seems really down, and has been doing strange things like giving his favourite things away. He recently told you that he thought that people he knew would be better off without him around, and that he'd thought about killing himself. After he tells you, he asks you not to tell anyone else about what he's said.

9 A kid in your class often gets completely ignored and occasionally teased and even bullied. No one will ever be seen talking to this person. The teachers don't seem to notice, and no one does anything to this kid when teachers are around.

10 A friend has started skipping a lot of school and seems pretty down.

11 Your friend has a parent with mental illness. From time to time, when the parent isn't doing well, your friend has to do everything at home. None of your other friends know about the situation. Your friend doesn't even know that you know. Your mom found out through a neighbour.

12 A classmate who is not really your friend, but is not friends with anyone else either, has started acting really strangely. Other kids have been laughing and making fun, but underneath you think this is a bit scary, and maybe the person is not doing this on purpose.

Adapted from Lesson 4 of Coping - *MindMatters*

Something is not quite right: Getting help early for mental illness*

You have a feeling that something is "not quite right" about the way someone close to you is behaving. You're worried, but you're not sure if it might be serious, or if moodiness, irritability and withdrawn behaviour is a stage they'll grow out of. Could drugs be involved? Do you think you might need a professional opinion to help you decide if there is a serious problem?

Getting help early

The chances are that there is not a serious problem, and that time, reassurance and support are all that are needed. However, if a mental illness is developing, then getting help early is very important.

Being unwell for a shorter time means less time lost as school or work and more time for relationships, experiences and activities which help us stay emotionally healthy.

Checklist #1 Difficult behaviour at home, at school or in the workplace:

Behaviour which is considered "normal", although difficult:

People may be:

☐ rude ☐ weepy ☐ thoughtless ☐ irritable ☐ argumentative ☐ over-sensitive

☐ over-emotional ☐ lazy ☐ withdrawn ☐ rebellious ☐ shy

These behaviours may also occur as a normal, brief reaction to stressful events such as:

☐ breakup of a close relationship ☐ moving ☐ divorce ☐ other family crisis

☐ death of a loved one ☐ other personal crisis ☐ exam failure ☐ physical illness

Probably no cause for serious concern, but…

It is often best to try not to over-react. Try to be as supportive as possible while waiting for the "bad patch" to pass. If the behaviour is too disruptive or is distressing to other people, or if the difficult behaviour lasts a long time, then you could seek professional counseling, help or advice. Talk it over with your family doctor, school counselor, community or mental health centre.

*Adapted from *MindMatters: Understanding Mental Illness,* Pg. 77-79

Checklist #2 –
What's the difference between just having a bad day and something potentially more serious?

Signs of Clinical Depression:

☐ Feeling miserable for at least 2 weeks

☐ Feeling like crying a lot of the time

☐ Not wanting to do anything, go anywhere, see anyone

☐ Having trouble concentrating or getting things done

☐ Feeling like you're operating in "slow-motion"

☐ Having trouble sleeping

☐ Feeling tired and lacking energy – being unable to get out of bed even after a full night's sleep

☐ Having a change in appetite

☐ Feeling like there's a "glass wall" between you and the rest of the world

☐ Feeling hopeless or thinking of suicide

☐ Always putting yourself down and thinking you're no good

If you often experience a number of these things, you may be depressed. Remember that you don't have to be alone with these feelings, and that depression is treatable!

Adapted from *MindMatters: Understanding Mental Illness,* Pg. 77-79

Checklist #3 – Behaviours which are considered ABNORMAL for that person, and may seriously affect other people.

People may:

- ☐ Withdraw completely from family, friends, and workmates

- ☐ Be afraid to leave the house (particularly during daylight hours)

- ☐ Sleep or eat poorly

- ☐ Sleep by day and stay awake at night, often pacing restlessly

- ☐ Be extremely occupied with a particular theme, for example, death, politics or religion

- ☐ Uncharacteristically neglect household or parental responsibilities, or personal appearance or hygiene

- ☐ Deteriorate in performance at school or work

- ☐ Have difficulty concentrating, following conversation or remembering things

- ☐ Talk about or write things that do not really make sense.

- ☐ Panic, be extremely anxious, or signficantly depressed and suicidal

- ☐ Lose variation in mood – be "flat" – lack emotional expression, for example, humour or friendliness

- ☐ Have marked changes in mood, from quiet to excited or agitated

- ☐ Hear voices that no one else can hear

- ☐ Believe, without reason, that others are plotting against, spying on, or following them, and be extremely angry or afraid of these people

- ☐ Believe that they are being harmed or asked to do things against their will, by, for instance, television, radio, aliens, God or the devil

- ☐ Believe they have special powers, for example, that they are important religious leaders, politicians or scientists

- ☐ Believe that their thoughts are being interfered with or that they can influence the thoughts of others

- ☐ Spend extravagant or unrealistic sums of money

Seek medical assessment as soon as possible These types of behaviours are much clearer signs that someone needs to be checked out, particularly if they have been present for several weeks. They may be only a minor disturbance, but a mental illness such as a psychotic disorder may be developing.

V

Make sure to emphasize that everyone has a personal responsibility to take action if a friend mentions thoughts of suicide. Young people should always share this information with a trusted adult – like a teacher, guidance counselor, coach, relative or parent – and never promise to keep the information secret.

Activity 3:   (10 mins.)

Support strategies*

Purpose:

• To provide students with strategies for supporting friends and others who are having trouble coping because of mental health problems or mental illness.

How-to:

1) Begin a discussion about the role that young people often play as supporters when they listen to their friends talk about their problems.

Ask students how they would like to be treated if they had a mental illness. Use the overhead as a starting point to encourage further discussion. Distribute photocopies of Activity 3 Support strategies and Recovery: What works? to each student. Read through the sheets with the class.

*Adapted from Lesson 4 of Coping - *MindMatters*.

Support Strategies –

Here are some strategies for supporting someone with a mental health problem/illness:

- Be supportive and understanding.

- Spend time with the person. Listen to him or her.

- Never underestimate the person's capacity to recover.

- Encourage the person to follow his or her treatment plan and to seek out support services. Offer to accompany them to appointments.

- Become informed about mental illness.

- Remember that even though your friend may be going through a hard time, they will recover. Stand by them.

- If you're planning an outing to the movies or the community centre, remember to ask your friend along. Keeping busy and staying in touch with friends will help your friend feel better, when they're ready.

- If you are a close friend or family member of someone who has a mental illness, make sure you get support as well. Crisis training, self-help and/or individual counseling will help you become a better support person.

- Put the person's life before your friendship. If you think the person needs help, especially if he or she mentions thoughts of suicide, don't keep it a secret – even if the person asked you to.

If a friend mentions thoughts of suicide or self harm, you NEED to tell his or her parents, a teacher, guidance councelor or someone else who can help. It's better to have a friend who's angry with you for a while than to keep their secret and live with knowing you could have helped, but remained quiet when your friend was in trouble.

Recovery – What helps people with mental illness get (and stay) better?

Recovery is an ongoing, slow process, and is different for each person. Research on recovery shows that there are a number of factors which people often mention are important:

- The presence of people who believe in and stand by the person who is in recovery.

- That person's ability to make their own choices about important things like treatment and housing.

Other factors that can support recovery include:

- Mutual support (self-help groups)

- Social opportunities (church groups; drop-in centres, volunteer work, participating in community life)

- Positive relationships (accepting and being accepted, family and friends and communicating with them in a positive way)

- Meaningful daily activity - Being able to work, go to school

- Medication (sticking with a treatment plan, working with doctors to find the best medications with the fewest side effects)

- Spirituality (involvement in a faith community or individual spiritual practice)

- Inner healing capacity and inner peace (finding a sense of meaning and purpose, even in suffering)

- Personal growth and development (hobbies, self education, taking control of one's life, exercise, personal goal setting)

- Self awareness (self-monitoring, recognizing when to seek help, recognizing one's accomplishments and accepting and/or learning from one's failures)

Deegan et. al., 2000, Canadian Mental Health Association, NS Division 1995

The importance of positive mental health

Overview:

What constitutes a mentally healthy person? Does everyone have mental health? In this module, students will explore these questions and will look at the impact of mental health on overall well-being. Through several group activities, students will also learn about the impact of stress, and will identify appropriate and effective coping strategies to deal with stress.

Learning Objectives:

- To describe the characteristics of an emotionally healthy person
- To demonstrate skills that enhance personal mental health, including stress management techniques

Major Concepts Addressed:

- Everyone has mental health that can be supported and promoted, regardless of whether or not they also have a mental illness
- Positive coping strategies can help everyone maintain and enhance their mental mealth

Materials Required:

- Handouts: Activity 1 Taking care of your mental health, Activity 3 Coping cards
- Flip chart paper and pens

In Advance:

- Photocopy handouts for Activity 1 Taking care of your mental health (one copy for each student) and Activity 3 Coping Cards (only one copy)
- Cut out Coping Cards

Teacher Preparation:

Read through all activities before class

MODULE 6

V

Websites such as the Canadian Mental Health Association's (www.cmha.ca) and the Centre for Addiction and Mental Health (CAMH) www.camh.net offer reliable and accessible information on many topics related to mental health and illness. Other websites specifically geared to youth are listed in the Resources section of this guide.

Activity 1: (5 mins.)

What do you think about mental health?

Purpose:

- To explore students' growing understanding of mental health, and its importance to each individual.
- To brainstorm about the kinds of things that contribute to positive mental health.

How to:

1) Ask students to brainstorm ideas of the kinds of things that keep people mentally healthy. Potential ideas are listed below:

   - think positive
   - organize your time
   - value yourself
   - eat right and exercise
   - try new things
   - get enough sleep
   - make plans
   - set realistic goals and work towards them
   - reward yourself
   - share concerns and worries with friends and family

2) Hand out photocopies of 'Taking care of your mental health' for students to keep.

Taking care of your mental health:

Achieving mental health is about striking a balance in the social, physical, spiritual, economic and mental aspects of our lives. Reaching a balance is a learning process and it is ongoing. At times, we may tip the balance too much in one direction and have to find our footing again. Our personal balance is highly individual, and our challenge is to stay mentally healthy by finding and keeping that balance.

Mental health and mental illness each run along a continuum. When our personal balance is off, either repeatedly or for long periods, we may eventually find ourselves moving closer along the continuum towards mental illness. While some people experience a sudden onset of symptoms of a mental illness, many mental health problems develop gradually. For example, you may hardly notice your anxiety turn to distress until, one day, you feel overwhelmed. To find out more about building healthy self-esteem, creating positive relationships, coping with change, and learning to manage stress, read the 10 tips below taken from the CMHA fact sheet Mental Health For Life, at www.ontario.cmha.ca/fact_sheets.asp?cID=3219

From nurturing relationships with family and friends, to identifying and dealing with situations that upset you – including stressful circumstances, such as the pressure of exams, a conflict at work, or a misunderstanding with a friend – you can take steps to improve and maintain your mental health throughout your life.

The Canadian Mental Health Association has <u>10 tips for mental health</u>:

1. Build a healthy self-esteem
2. Receive as well as give
3. Create positive parenting and family relationships
4. Make friends who count
5. Figure out your priorities
6. Get involved
7. Learn to manage stress effectively
8. Cope with changes that affect you
9. Deal with your emotions
10. Have a spirituality to call your own

MODULE 6

Taking care of your mental health
Consider these key characteristics when assessing your own mental health:

Ability to enjoy life – Can you live in the moment and appreciate the "now"? Are you able to learn from the past and plan for the future without dwelling on things you can't change or predict?

Resilience – Are you able to bounce back from hard times? Can you manage the stress of a serious life event without losing your optimism and sense of perspective?

Balance – Are you able to juggle the many aspects of your life? Can you recognize when you might be devoting too much time to one aspect, at the expense of others? Are you able to make changes to restore balance when necessary?

Self-actualization – Do you recognize and develop your strengths so that you can reach your full potential?

Flexibility – Do you feel, and express, a range of emotions? When problems arise, can you change your expectations – of life, others, yourself – to solve the problem and feel better?

You can gauge your mental health by thinking about how you coped with a recent difficulty. Did you feel there was no way out of the problem and that life would never be normal again? Were you unable to carry on with work or school? With time, were you able to enjoy your life, family and friendships?
Were you able to regain your balance and look forward to the future?

Taking the pulse of mental health brings different results for everyone; it's unique to each individual. By reflecting on these characteristics, you can recognize your strengths, and identify areas where your level of mental fitness could be improved.

Activity 2:   (15 mins.)

What do we mean by "Stress?"*

Purpose:

- To identify different kinds of stress and the impact that stress can have on overall well-being
- To give examples of stressors commonly experienced by young people, and explore different coping strategies and positive ways of dealing with stress

How to:

1) Ask students to imagine that they are about to explain to an alien what human beings mean by stress. Ask them to form pairs and talk with their partner and develop a definition, e.g. "stress is when…" and write their ideas down in point form.

2) Ask each pair to share their definitions, and write them on the board as they read them aloud.

3) Ask students what they notice about what stress means to different people.

4) Ask students to brainstorm about the different kinds of stressors. Use the list below as a guide to make sure all areas are mentioned. Write their responses on the board

   Different kinds of stressors:
   - Physical stressors (e.g. injury, illness, fatigue, hunger, lack of shelter)
   - Social stressors (e.g. arguments, rejection, embarrassment)
   - Intellectual stressors (e.g. mental fatigue, lack of understanding)
   - Emotional stressors (e.g. death of a close friend or family member)
   - Spiritual Stressors (e.g. guilt, moral conflicts, lack of sense of purpose)

cont.>

*adapted from *MindMatters, Coping*, pg. 23

V

Introduce the idea that stress can be seen either as a challenge or an opportunity, or as a nightmare or trap. Tell students that people who can imagine or visualize themselves handling their challenges or stresses in a positive way, with an image of themselves having some power or control, are able to bounce back more easily after difficult times. Provide the example of professional athletes, who often use mental pictures to visualize themselves conquering a challenge. Explain to students that this technique can also work for the rest of us – that we can all work at inventing or imagining pictures of ourselves succeeding, and this can help us to do our best in a situation where we fear failure, embarrassment or hard work. Explain that research has shown that people who can learn to visualize themselves succeeding are more likely to actually succeed.

Activity 2:

How to (cont.)

5) Divide students into groups of four or five. Ask each group to brainstorm around the following question: "What are some of the stresses and challenges people around your age face?"

   Circulate around the room as the students are brainstorming in their groups, and use the probes below if they need help or direction

   - What sorts of stresses in the physical environment can directly affect how you feel either physically or emotionally?

   - What sorts of stresses or challenges can happen to relationships or between people?

   - What kinds of happenings or events can cause stress (e.g. family breakup, transitions like leaving school or moving, illness, end of a close relationship, etc.)

   - What are some of the fears, anxieties or thoughts that can get people feeling stressed?

6) As the groups report back, ask several students to record the brainstorm results on flip chart paper. Explain that this list will be used later, in the next activity.

Activity 3 : (15 mins.)

How do you cope?*

Purpose:

- To describe a range of coping strategies to deal with stressful and challenging situations
- To identify some of students' own preferred coping strategies, and examine the effectiveness of different strategies

How to:

1) Remind students that in the previous activity they identified the kinds of things people can feel stressed-out about, and some of the thoughts and feelings they can have when faced with challenging and stressful situations.

2) Ask students to get into pairs or groups of three, and ask them to share examples of things they like to do when they feel stressed or overworked. Ask a student in each group to write down at least one of the coping strategies discussed. To prepare for the next part of the activity, while students are busy in their groups, stick up one piece of paper in each corner of the room, with the words "Helpful", "Not much use", Useless" and "Harmful" written on them.

3) Explain to the class that in this activity you'll be examining coping strategies, or things that people do in response to stress or challenge. Point out that there is a huge range of possible coping strategies, that it's different for each individual, varies in terms of a person's culture, religious background, gender, etc. and that there is no one right way of coping. Explain that people who cope effectively often have a whole range of different strategies that they use, and that people often learn about coping by watching what their friends and family do.

4) Have students come back together and arrange themselves in a circle. Ask those who recorded their group's coping strategies to put the paper on the floor in the middle of the circle, and spread Coping Cards into the pile, face down. Ask each student to choose two cards or strategies offered by the students.

5) Ask students to choose one of the cards and hold it up at chest height so that it can be read by others.

cont.>

---

* Adapted from *MindMatters: Coping*, pg 34.

MODULE 6

Activity 3: How do you cope?*

How to (cont.)

6) Explain to the class that you will describe a situation of potential stress or challenge. Students will then be asked to move to a defined area of the room according to whether they think their coping strategy would be helpful, not much use, useless or harmful.

7) Describe the scenario, choosing either from the brainstormed list that the students came up with, or from the suggestions below:

   • faced with a big exam
   • dealing with separation of parents
   • dealing with death of someone close

8) When the students have grouped, have them compare and comment on their choices. Ask them to put their other coping card on top and regroup if they think this card belongs to a different category.

9) Play a few rounds of the game to emphasize the point that different situations may call for different coping strategies. Remind students that there are no right or wrong answers, and that sometimes the most important coping strategy can involve getting help or support for yourself or someone else.

---

* Adapted from *MindMatters: Coping*, pg 34.

MODULE 6

Coping Cards

Withdraw – not mix with other people	Think positive about how it will turn out
Play computer games	Worry
Visit a favourite person	See a counsellor
Eat more	Eat junk food
Quit (the job, the team…)	Sleep more
Avoid or put off something you have to do	Go for a run
Prioritize (put the most important things first)	Party/socialize
Fantasize - daydream an escape	Run away
Plan – figure out how to do it	Get sick
Start a fight	Blame someone else

MODULE 6

Coping Cards

Blame yourself	Smoke cigarettes
Ask for help	Go out
Talk it over	Complain
Eat less	Change direction
Have a shower	Go to bed early
Drink alcohol	Exercise
Work harder	Stay out late
Meditate	Listen to music
Pretend it's OK	Call friends
Watch television	Write about it

Coping Cards

Cook something	Sleep less
Walk the dog	Go shopping
Pray	Draw or paint
Take a day off	Tidy up
Take risks	Make something
Problem-solve	Find new friends
Cry	Joke or laugh
Set goals	Go for a swim
Play sports	

V

At least some of the student's answers should be different now that they have learned more about mental illness. Even if some students' attitudes have not changed within the span of this unit, the knowledge they have gained may influence their opinions about how people who have a mental illness should be treated. Notice that the discussion questions above do not ask students to divulge their answers. Because of the potentially sensitive nature of the questions, students may be uncomfortable sharing what they wrote. Use your judgment in discussing responses to specific questions. The discussion will need to be handled with sensitivity because students may bring up personal experiences or stories. You might want to ask the school guidance counselor or other support staff to be present, or to help facilitate the discussion.

Optional Activity: (15 mins.)

What do you think about mental illness now?*

Purpose:

- To provide students with an opportunity to reflect on the changes in their knowledge and attitudes about mental illness from the first module.

How to:

1) Hand out a copy of the "What do you think" questionnaire to each student and give them 5 minutes to answer the questions

2) After students have answered the questions, give each student their copy of the questionnaire that they completed in Module 2. Ask students to compare the answers they just wrote with the answers they wrote in the earlier module. Give students a few minutes to compare their responses, reminding them that they should only be looking at their own answers. Ask students whether their answers are different today from when they answered the questions in Module 2, and if so, how they are different.

3) Conduct a brief group discussion around students' responses. Use the following questions as a guide:

   - If your answers were different today, why do you think they were different?

   - Does learning about mental illness make a difference? Why?

   - Do you think you would react differently now to someone who has mental illness compared to your reaction before you completed this unit?

Glossary*

* Definitions reproduced with permission form *The Science of Mental Illness Curriculum Supplement*. http://science-education.nih.gov/customers.nsf/ MSMental. Some have been modified for clarity.

Acute: Refers to an illness or condition that has a rapid onset, marked intensity and short duration.

Acute Stress Disorder (ASD): Persistence of substantial stress induced symptoms beyond usually expected levels and time.

Antidepressant: A medication used to treat depression.

Anorexia Nervosa (AN): is characterized by excessive preoccupation with body weight control, a distrubed body image, an intense fear of gaining weight and a refusal to maintain a minimally normal weight.

Anxiety: An abnormal sense of fear, nervousness and apprehension about something that might happen in the future.

Anxiety Disorder: A group of illnesses that fill people's lives with overwhelming anxieties and fears that are chronic and unremitting. Anxiety disorders include panic disorder, obsessive-compulsive disorder, post-traumatic stress disorder, phobias and generalized anxiety disorder.

Attention Deficit Hyperactivity Disorder (ADHD): A mental illness characterized by an impaired ability to regulate activity level (hyperactivity), attend to tasks (inattention) and inhibit behaviour (impulsivity). For a diagnosis of ADHD, the behaviours must appear before an individual reaches age seven, continue for at least six months, be more frequent than in other children of the same age, and cause impairment in at least two areas of life (school, home, work or social functioning).

Bipolar Disorder: A mood disorder in which a person alternates between episodes of major depression and mania (periods of abnormally and persistently elevated mood). Also referred to as manic depression.

Bulimia Nervosa (BN): is characterized by regular and recurrent binge eating, and by frequent and in appropriate behaviours designed to prevent weight gain.

Chronic: refers to an illness, disorder, or condition that persists over a long period of time.

Cognition: Conscious mental activity that informs a person about his or her environment. Cognitive actions include: perceiving, thinking, reasoning, judging, problem solving and remembering.

Cognitive Behaviour Therapy (CBT): Psychological treatment that includes changing how people think about their past, present and future.

Delusion: A false belief that persists even when a person has evidence that the belief is not true.

Depression: (depressive disorders) A group of diseases including major depressive disorder (commonly referred to as depression), dysthymia and bipolar disorder (manic depression). *See bipolar disorder, dysthymia and major depressive disorder.*

Disorder: An abnormality in mental or physical health. In this guide, it is used as a synonym for illness.

Dysthymia (also referred to as Dysthymic Disorder (DD)): A depressive disorder that is less severe than major depressive disorder but is more persistent. In children and adolescents, dysthymia lasts for an average of four years.

Electroconvulsive Therapy (ECT): An effective treatment for severe depression that is used only when people do not respond to medications and psychotherapy. ECT involves passing a low-voltage electric current through the brain. The person is under anesthesia at the time of treatment. ECT is not commonly used in children and adolescents.

General Anxiety Disorder (GAD): Excessive anxiety and worry occuring for an extended period of time about several different things. This persistent apprehension, worry and anxiety causes sustantial emotional distress and physical symptoms and leads to functional impairment.

Hallucination: The perception of something, such as a sound or visual image, that is not actually present other than in the mind.

Major Depressive Disorder (MDD): A mood disorder commonly referred to as depression. Depression is more than simply being sad; to be diagnosed with depression, a person must have five or more characteristic symptoms nearly every day for a two-week period.

Mania: Feelings of intense mental and physical hyperactivity, elevated mood and agitation.

Manic Depression: See bipolar disorder.

Mental illness: A brain health condition that changes a person's thinking, feelings or behaviour (or all three) and that causes the person substantial distress and difficulty in functioning.

Obsessive Compulsive Disorder (OCD): An anxiety disorder in which a person experiences recurrent unwanted thoughts or rituals that the individual cannot control. A person who has OCD may be plagued by persistent, unwelcome thoughts or images or by the urgent need to engage in certain rituals such as hand washing or checking.

Panic Disorder (PD): An anxiety disorder in which people have feelings of terror, rapid heart beat and rapid breathing that strike suddenly and repeatedly with no warning. A person who has panic disorder cannot predict when an attack will occur and may develop intense anxiety between episodes, worrying when and where the next one will strike.

Phobia: An intense fear of something that poses little or no actual danger. Examples of phobias include fear of closed-in-places, heights, escalators, tunnels, highway driving, water, flying, spiders and dogs.

Post Traumatic Stress Disorder (PTSD): develops after a trauma occurs that was either experienced or witnessed. It involves the development of psychological/physical reactions related to the experience such as recurrent, intrusive and distressing recollections of the event.

Psychiatrist: A medical doctor (M.D.) who specializes in treating mental diseases. A psychiatrist evaluates a person's mental health along with his or her physical health and prescribes medications.

Psychiatry: The branch of medicine that deals with identifying, studying and treating mental, emotional and behavioural disorders.

Psychologist: A mental health professional who has received specialized training in the study of the mind and emotions. A psychologist usually has an advanced degree such as a PhD.

Psychosis: A serious mental disorder in which a person loses contact with reality and experiences hallucinations and/or delusions.

Recovery: Recovery from mental illness refers to a person's improved capacity to lead a fulfilled life that is not dominated by illness and treatment. Recovery does not always mean that symptoms go away completely, or that people no longer need medication or support services. Recovery is defined differently for each individual, but most often means that a person has the capacity to find purpose and enjoyment in their life despite their illness.

Relapse: The recurrence of symptoms of an illness.

Schizophrenia (SCZ): A psychotic disorder characterized in the active phase by hallucinations, delusions, disorganized thoughts/speech, disorganized or catatonic behavior, and apathy. Schizophrenia is an extremely complex mental disorder; in fact it is probably many illnesses masquerading as one. A biochemical imbalance is believed to cause symptoms. which usually develop in the late teens or early twenties.

Serotonin: A neurotransmitter that regulates many functions, including mood, appetite and sensory perception.

Stigma: Stigma is the use of negative labels to identify a person living with mental illness.

Symptom: Something which indicates the presence of an illness.

About Laing House

Laing House is a community support centre for young adults, ages 17-24, who are living with serious mental illnesses such as psychosis or mood disorders. Launched in January 2001, it is located in a refurbished Victorian house in downtown Halifax. Laing House starts with a belief that young people have an array of talents and strengths which, when supported, point them towards recovery. Youth are invited to participate - as members of Laing House – in a welcoming, respectful and collaborative environment. Involvement is voluntary and referrals can come from the young person, a family member, community agency, or mental health professional. Laing House is unique in Canada.

Laing House's mission is "to prepare youth living with mental illness for healthy futures".

Laing House seeks to reduce isolation, to address needs in relation to returning to school, seeking employment, re-establishing a peer group, and finding a place to live. The programs focus on these core areas, while allowing youth to gain the confidence they need to be healthy and productive. Already, more than 200 young people have found their way to Laing House, where a team of peers and professional staff provide supports.

Youth and staff build relationships and work together to create personal development, community education and advocacy programs. These experiences and opportunities provide youth with support and resources to resume educational and vocational paths, find safe housing, and become contributing members of their natural communities.
http://www.lainghouse.org

Laing House
1225 Barrington Street
Halifax, NS B3J 1Y2
Telephone: (902) 473-7743
Email: contact@lainghouse.org

Template - Community Mental Health Resources

The following mental health related resources are available in many communities. Find out the contact information for these resources in your community and distribute to students.

Kids Help Phone – 1-800-668-6868

Kids Help Phone is Canada's only 24-hour, national bilingual telephone counseling service for children and youth. Provides counseling directly to children and youth directly between the ages of 4 and 19 years and helps adults aged 20 and over to find the counseling services they need.

Parents, teachers and any other concerned adults are welcome to call for information and referral services at any time.

Local Distress lines _____

Local Mental Health Organizations_____

Canadian Mental Health Association

For information about the CMHA Branch in your area, please see the CMHA National website at **www. cmha.ca**

Schizophrenia Society

For information about your local Schizophrenia Society Chapter, please see their website at **www. schizophrenia.ca**

Local Community Mental Health Clinic _____

Local Community Health Centre_____

Local Hospital_____

For more information

Websites and other resources for teachers –
Further information on mental health problems and mental illness

Canadian Mental Health Association
www.cmha.ca

CMHA National has a comprehensive range of information available to download from their website, including a complete series of pamphlets with vital information on mental health and mental illness.

Additionally, you will find many resources pertaining to mental health and high school for teachers, parents and students at www.cmha.ca/highschool

American Academy of Child and Adolescent Psychiatry
http://www.aacap.org/

The AACAP website contains a wide range of information on childhood and adolescent mental health and illness geared toward different audiences, including educators and parents.

Parents and Teachers as Allies
http://www.nami.org/Content/ContentGroups/Youth/Parents_and_Teachers_as_Allies.htm

by Joyce Burland, Ph.D., National Director, NAMI Education, Training and Peer Support Center, Second Edition, 2003. Available through NAMI, c/o Lynne Saunders, Colonial Place Three, 2017 Wilson Blvd. Suite 300. Arlington, VA. 22201-3042 or by fax (703) 524-9094. ($1.00 per copy)

A useful guide that can help parents and teachers identify the key warning signs of early-onset mental illness among children and adolescents. It focuses on specific, age-related symptoms of mental illness in young people, which may differ from adult criteria for diagnosis.

National Institute for Mental Health (NIMH)
http://www.nimh.nih.gov/

The NIMH website contains up-to date and reliable information about a wide range of issues relating to mental health and illness across the lifespan.

Classroom Resources

When Something's Wrong: Ideas for Teachers with Troubled Students
http://www.cprf.ca/publication/WSW_order.pdf

A quick reference source of useful classroom strategies to help elementary and secondary school teachers and administrators understand and assist students with mood, behaviour or thinking disorders.

Available from the Canadian Psychiatric Research Foundation
($10 including shipping and handing)

Eliminating Barriers for Learning: Social and Emotional factors that Enhance Secondary Education.
Substance Abuse and Mental Health Services Administration, 2004. U.S. Department of Health and Human Services

http://allmentalhealth.samhsa.gov/schools.html

Eliminating barriers for learning is a packaged continuing education program for secondary school teachers that focuses on mental health issues in the classroom.

MindMatters: A Mental Health Promotion Resource for Secondary Schools
http://cms.curriculum.edu.au/mindmatters/

A resource and professional development program to support Australian secondary schools in promoting and protecting the social and emotional wellbeing of members of school communities.

Reaching Out
http://www.schizophrenia.ca/reachingout/

A complete, easy to teach, bilingual educational program specially created for Canadian youth. The program includes classroom activities and a video which provide information on psychosis and schizophrenia.

The Science of Mental Illness – National Institute of Mental Health Curriculum Supplement Series
http://science-education.nih.gov/customers.nsf/MSMental

In this supplement designed to address science curriculum for Grades 6-8, students gain insight into the biological basis of mental illnesses and how scientific evidence and research can help us understand its causes and lead to treatments and, ultimately, cures.

Talking About Mental Illness
http://www.camh.net/education/Resources_teachers_schools/TAMI/index.html

The Centre for Addiction and Mental Health's Talking About Mental Illness Teacher's Resource Guide contains all of the information, support and tools teachers will need to implement the program in their classroom. The awareness program is focused on combating stigma, and has been proven to bring about positive change in students' knowledge and attitudes about mental illness.

Youth Engagement through Schools – Peer Helper programs
http://www.safehealthyschools.org/youth/peer_helper_programs.htm

This webpage is a good source of information on peer-helper programs which address a variety of academic, recreational, social and other health needs. The page also contains a number of links for more information on setting up peer helper programs.

Information geared to young people

Psychosis Sucks
http://www.psychosissucks.ca/epi/

This site contains valuable information for youth in the importance of early intervention in psychosis. It includes information on warning signs and how to get help, along with personal stories and accounts of recovery.

Mind your Mind
http://www.mindyourmind.ca/

Mindyourmind.ca is an award winning site for youth by youth. This is a place where youth can get information, resources and the tools to help manage stress, crisis and mental health problems.

General Mental Health Websites

Teen Mental Health (Sun Life Financial Chair in Adolescent Mental Health IWK/Dalhousie University)
http://www.teenmentalhealth.org/

Canadian Health Network:
http://www.canadian-health-network.ca/1mental_health.html

Canadian Mental Health Association, National Office:
http://www.cmha.ca/

Centre for Addiction and Mental Health:
http://www.camh.net

Health Canada, Mental Health Web sit:
http://www.hc-sc.gc.ca/hppb/mentalhealth/index.html

National Alliance on Mental Illness (USA):
http://www.nami.org/

SAMHSA's National Mental Health Information Centre (USA):
http://nmhicstore.samhsa.gov/publications/Publications_browse.asp?ID=176&Topic=Mental+Illnesses
%2FDisorders

MindMatters: A Mental Health Promotion Resource for Secondary Schools (Australia):
http://www.mindmatters.edu.au/default.asp

Continuing Medical Education (CME) mental health information (USA):
http://www.cmellc.com/topics/

Module 1: The stigma of mental illness

Talking about Mental Illness: Teachers' Resource
http://www.camh.net/education/Resources_teachers_schools/TAMI/tami_teachersresource.html

SAMHSA's National Mental Health Information Centre (USA):
http://nmhicstore.samhsa.gov/publications/Publications_browse.asp?ID=58&Topic=Stigma

The World Psychiatric Association program to fight stigma due to schizophrenia:
http://www.openthedoors.com/

Confront the stigma of mental illness:
http://www.letsfacethis.ca/

A report on mental illness in Canada (including "fighting with stigma"):
http://www.cmha.ca/bins/content_page.asp?cid=4-42-215

Module 2: Understanding mental health and mental illness

Teen Mental Health (Sun Life Financial Chair in Adolescent Mental Health IWK/Dalhousie University)
http://www.teenmentalhealth.org

National Institute of Mental Health Curriculum Supplement (USA):
http://science-education.nih.gov/customers.nsf/MSMental

Module 3: Information on specific mental illnesses

Mood Disorders:
Moods Magazine: http://www.moodsmag.com/

Sun Financial Chair in Adolescent Mental Health:
http://www.teenmentalhealth.org/pros_courses.php

Mood Disorders Association of Ontario (MDAO):
http://www.mooddisorders.on.ca/

Depression and Bipolar Support Alliance (USA): http://www.dbsalliance.org/site/
PageServer?pagename=home

Bipolar Disorder Information Centre (USA):
http://www.mhsource.com/bipolar/index.html

Schizophrenia:
Schizophrenia Society of Canada:
http://www.schizophrenia.ca/Reaching.htm

Schizophrenia.com:
http://www.schizophrenia.com/

Schizophrenia Digest:
http://www.schizophreniadigest.com/

Anxiety disorder:
Anxiety Disorders Association of Canada:
http://www.anxietycanada.ca/

Obsessive-Compulsive Foundation:
http://www.ocfoundation.org/

Anxiety Disorders Association of America:
http://www.adaa.org/

Eating Disorder:
National Eating Disorder Information Centre:
http://www.nedic.ca

Eating Disorders Awareness and Prevention (USA):
http://www.edap.org

Bulimia Anorexia Nervosa Association:
http://www.bana.ca

Psychosis Sucks:
http://www.psychosissucks.ca/epi

Module 4: Experiences of mental illness

Talking about Mental Illness: Teachers' Resource
http://www.camh.net/education/Resources_teachers_schools/TAMI/tami_teachersresource.html

Module 5: Seeking help and finding support

The Self-Help Resource Centre of Ontario: http://www.selfhelp.on.ca/

Treatment of Bipolar Disorder: A guide for patients and families: http://www.psychguides.com

Focus Adolescent Services: Warning Signs, Information, Getting Help: http://www.focusas.com/Depression.html

Eclipse Depression and Manic Depression Support Group: http://comdir.bfree.on.ca/eclipse/

Support programs by National Alliance on Mental Illness (NAMI): http://www.nami.org/Template.cfm?section=Find_Support

Psychosis Sucks: http://www.psychosissucks.ca/epi

Mind your Mind: http://www.mindyourmind.ca/

Youth Engagement through Schools – Peer Helper programs:
http://www.safehealthyschools.org/youth/peer_helper_programs.htm

MyHealth Magazine: http://www.myhealthmagazine.net/

YouthNet Ottawa
http://www.youthnet.on.ca

Youth Net Montréal
http://www.ra-yn.com

Youth Net Grey Bruce
http://www.youthnetgb.ca

Youth Net Halton
http://www.region.halton.on.ca/health/programs/mentalhealth/youth_net

Youth Net Hamilton
http://www.hamiltonyouthnet.ca

Youth Net Peel
http://www.youthnet.cmhapeel.ca

Youth Space, Victoria BC
http://youthspace.ca/

Youth One, Edmonton AB
http://www.youthone.com/

Here to Help, BC
http://www.heretohelp.bc.ca/

Module 6: The importance of positive mental health

World Health Organization:
http://www.who.int/mental_health/en/

Wellness Recovery Action Plan (WRAP):
www.mentalhealthrecovery.com/

Stand Up for Mental Health
www.standupformentalhealth.com

Grip on Life
http://www.griponlife.ca/

NOTES

CPSIA information can be obtained at www.ICGtesting.com
Printed in the USA
LVOW10s1948291014

411099LV00007B/606/P